STAR WARS®

REVENGE OF THE SITH™
THE VISUAL DICTIONARY

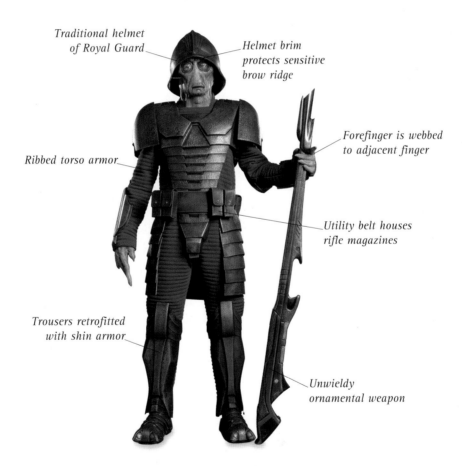

Traditional helmet of Royal Guard

Helmet brim protects sensitive brow ridge

Ribbed torso armor

Forefinger is webbed to adjacent finger

Utility belt houses rifle magazines

Trousers retrofitted with shin armor

Unwieldy ornamental weapon

NEIMOIDIAN WARRIOR

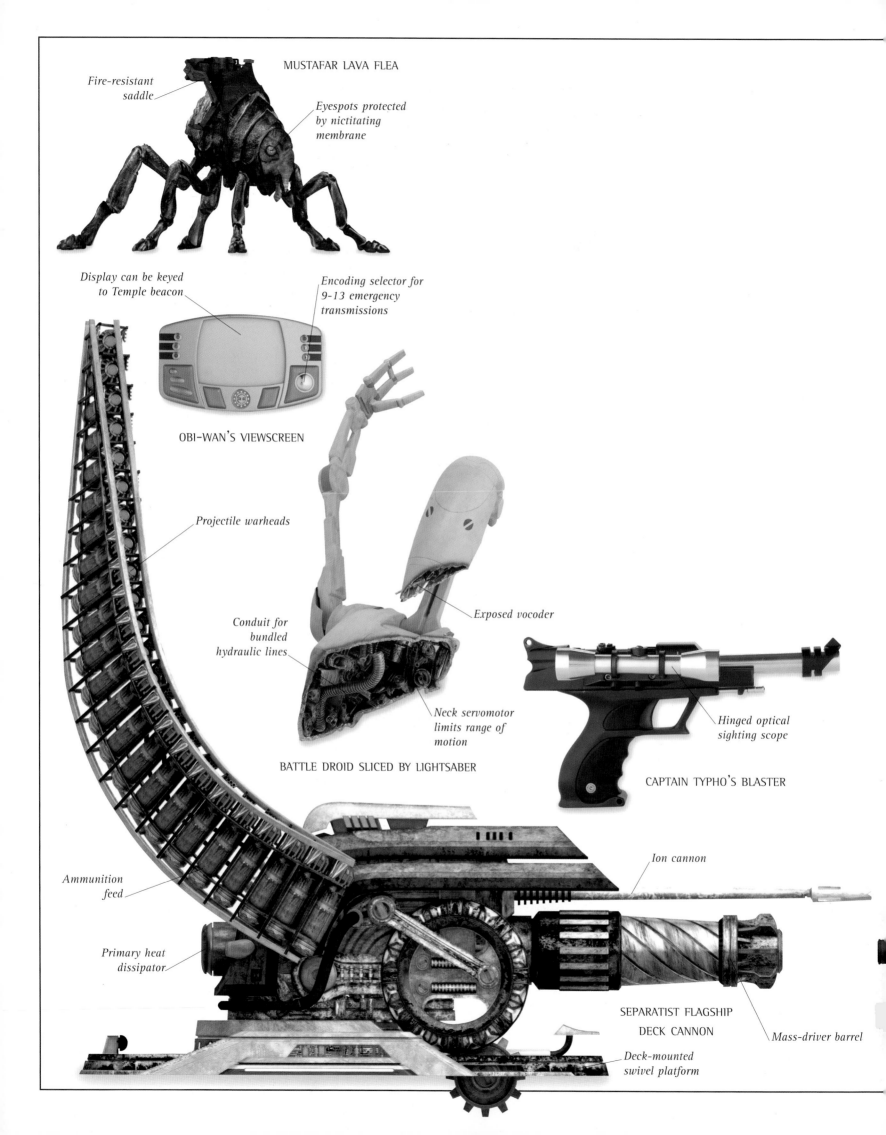

MUSTAFAR LAVA FLEA

Fire-resistant saddle

Eyespots protected by nictitating membrane

Display can be keyed to Temple beacon

Encoding selector for 9-13 emergency transmissions

OBI-WAN'S VIEWSCREEN

Projectile warheads

Conduit for bundled hydraulic lines

Exposed vocoder

Neck servomotor limits range of motion

BATTLE DROID SLICED BY LIGHTSABER

Hinged optical sighting scope

CAPTAIN TYPHO'S BLASTER

Ammunition feed

Primary heat dissipator

Ion cannon

SEPARATIST FLAGSHIP
DECK CANNON

Mass-driver barrel

Deck-mounted swivel platform

STAR WARS®

REVENGE OF THE SITH™
THE VISUAL DICTIONARY

Written by JAMES LUCENO

Special fabrications by ROBERT E. BARNES & JOHN GOODSON
New photography by ALEX IVANOV

Padawan braid has been ritually clipped

Jedi tunic

Utility pouch medkit

Synthleather surcoat

Field combat trousers

Tall travel boots

OBI-WAN KENOBI VERSUS
ANAKIN SKYWALKER

Ablative hull plates

KASHYYYK
ESCAPE POD

Transparisteel viewport

www.starwars.com LUCAS BOOKS DK www.dk.com

Contents

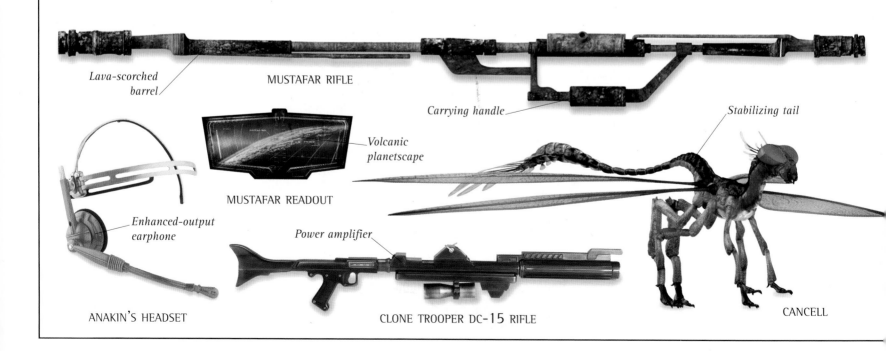

Lava-scorched barrel

MUSTAFAR RIFLE

Carrying handle

Stabilizing tail

Volcanic planetscape

MUSTAFAR READOUT

Enhanced-output earphone

Power amplifier

ANAKIN'S HEADSET

CLONE TROOPER DC-15 RIFLE

CANCELL

Introduction

STAR WARS: REVENGE OF THE SITH is at once the concluding chapter to events that have shaped the Prequel Trilogy—the era of the Republic—and a tragic prologue to the Dark Times—the 19-year period that witnesses the consolidation of power by Sith Lords Sidious and his pieced-together executioner, Darth Vader. Detailed in this Visual Dictionary are the key players in the fall of the Jedi Order, the ascendancy of the dark side of the Force, and the emergence of the dreaded Empire, founded on a mad lust for power and fortified by weapons the likes of which the galaxy has never seen. Brought to life in film stills and original art are the exotic locations that serve as stages for the final act, the hardware of galactic warfare, and profiles of the many subsidiary characters caught up in this numbing climax.

Revenge of the Sith is a tale forged in chaos, informed by deceit, betrayal, heartbreak, and the death of heroes. A story almost 30 years in the making, and one that will be told and retold here, and in galaxies far, far away. . . .

Galactic War

For THREE YEARS the Clone Wars have raged across the stars. In deep space and on a host of disparate worlds, the forces of the Republic and those of the Confederacy of Independent Systems (CIS) battle for supremacy. On one side stands a droid army led by a former Jedi named Count Dooku; on the other, an army of cloned soldiers led by the Jedi themselves, the galaxy's one-time guardians of peace. Few can explain why the conflict began, and fewer still understand what is at risk. In fact, the war is being waged by advocates of the dark side of the Force against those who call the Force their ally.

Coruscant

The varied denizens of Coruscant experienced the war from a safe distance, confident in the belief that Supreme Chancellor Palpatine could keep the fighting confined to the outer systems. But in such a conflict no world can remain untouched. So, finally, the war stabs even at the galactic capital itself, with a daring move by the Separatist forces, led by General Grievous, to abduct the Supreme Chancellor, raising the stakes to higher than they have ever been.

Above Coruscant, Republic and Separatist warships attack each other, after Grievous's MagnaGuards and battle droids have abducted Palpatine. Anakin and Obi-Wan Kenobi speed to Palpatine's rescue.

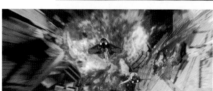

Utapau

An Outer Rim world of vast, arid plains and immense sinkholes, Utapau is a peaceful planet with few ties to either the Republic or the CIS. But, like Coruscant, the planet cannot escape the long reach of the war, and finds itself dragged to the forefront when droid forces under General Grievous's command invade and occupy. The Pau'an and Utai populations know that the liberation of their planet is in the hands of the Jedi Knights.

Kashyyyk

For countless millennia the skillful and resourceful Wookiees have lived in harmony with the towering wroshyr trees that dominate Kashyyyk's lush forests. But the Clone Wars bring changes even here, first with an invasion by Trandoshan slavers in league with the Separatists, then by legions of battle droids dispatched by Grievous to subjugate the entire planet.

Polarized T-visor
reduces glare

Battle-damaged
chest plastron

Cooling
backpack
turbine

Mustafar

The sulphurous skies
of Mustafar are filled
with fire and ash and
its craggy surface is
slagged by ceaseless floes of lava.
This remote planet is the last in a long
list chosen by Darth Sidious to serve as
a sanctuary for the hounded members
of the Separatist Council. On hellish
Mustafar the final acts of the Sith
plot will be played out, resulting in
the deaths of enemies, the
deaths of friends—and,
ultimately, the death of love.

Kubazian skirt

Standard
DC-15
blaster has a
folding stock

CLONE TROOPER
Symbol of the
Grand Army of the
Republic, the clone
trooper has become a
ubiquitous presence on
embattled worlds
throughout the galaxy.
In the grim theater that
is the Clone War, the
trooper is also a mindless
actor in a diabolical plot
to topple the galaxy
into darkness.

MUSTAFARIAN

In service to the long-snouted aliens who oversee
the Separatists' smelting facilities on Mustafar, agile
lava fleas leap across the fiery surface.

Anakin Skywalker

As THE CLONE TROOPER has become the emblem for the Grand Army of the Republic, Anakin Skywalker—dashing pilot and audacious Jedi Knight—has become the symbol of the Jedi Order and poster boy of the entire war effort. Praised in public by Supreme Chancellor Palpatine, applauded by the Senate, glorified on the HoloNet News, the "Hero With No Fear" is held by many to be the warrior-savior of the Republic. It is therefore only fitting that Anakin should rescue Supreme Chancellor Palpatine from the evil clutches of General Grievous aboard the giant flagship as it attempts to flee Coruscant.

Electrostatic fingertips allow some feeling

Ideal for outwitting the in-close weaponry of Grievous's flagship, *Invisible Hand*, Anakin's Jedi Interceptor slips along its turreted hull and infiltrates a docking bay.

Due to communication blunders among Republic forces, Grievous's flagship is blown in half with Palpatine aboard. Anakin and R2-D2 guide what remains of the ship to a controlled crash on Coruscant.

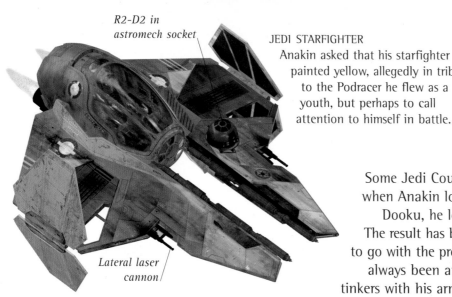

Ribbing and clamps ensure tight fit

Armored shielding bulks glove and protects electromotive lines

Alloy ligaments provide pronation and supination

Electrodrivers for pistons

Glove auto-seal

ANAKIN'S GLOVE

R2-D2 in astromech socket

JEDI STARFIGHTER
Anakin asked that his starfighter be painted yellow, allegedly in tribute to the Podracer he flew as a youth, but perhaps to call attention to himself in battle.

Lateral laser cannon

Interface modules link prosthesis to surviving nerves

Cyborg Limb

Some Jedi Council members believe that when Anakin lost his right arm to Count Dooku, he lost some of his humanity. The result has been a chip on his shoulder to go with the prosthesis. In fact, Anakin has always been at ease with technology, and tinkers with his arm as he does his starfighter.

Even though Anakin is envious of Obi-Wan's place on the Jedi Council, they remain the best of friends and the most dynamic of Jedi partners, especially during the Outer Rim sieges.

Anakin believes that the political decisions should be made quickly and decisively. He is free to air his convictions to Supreme Chancellor Palpatine, who is a mentor to him in the ways of the real world.

Gauntlet worn in combat

Synthleather surcoat

Aggressive stance

Chosen One?

Torn by a desire to accomplish great things, Anakin is fearful of change. While he is generally believed to be the Chosen One alluded to in an ancient Jedi prophecy, Anakin frequently finds his hands tied, in the same way that the Senate binds the hands of Supreme Chancellor Palpatine. Nevertheless, he is determined to honor Obi-Wan, and to live up to the title the Jedi have seen fit to bestow upon him.

Utility pouch for emergency rations

Anakin hasn't seen Padmé—or Coruscant—in almost five months. Their forbidden marriage is yet another lie Anakin has had to maintain since the start of the Clone Wars—a secret he is reluctant to share even with Palpatine, much less with Obi-Wan.

Double-Agent

When Palpatine appoints Anakin to the Jedi High Council to serve as his voice, the Council counters by ordering Anakin to spy on the Supreme Chancellor. In addition, the Council withholds from Anakin the title of Master, despite his accomplishments and his mastery of the Force. Discouraged to learn that the Jedi are not above duplicity, Anakin no longer feels guilty about the fact that he has kept secrets from them.

Tunic apron

Military grade trousers

Grappling hook and line

MUSTAFAR
On Mustafar, Anakin's love for Padmé and Obi-Wan mutates to hatred when he convinces himself that his wife and his former Master have betrayed him. A Sith now, having accepted Darth Sidious as his Master and Darth Vader as his name, Anakin shows no remorse in Force-choking Padmé, and engaging Obi-Wan in a duel to the death.

DATA FILE

◆ Anakin's facial scar is a reminder of his encounter with Dooku-trained Asajj Ventress.

◆ Anakin was named a Jedi Knight after his actions on the planet Praesitlyn, where he almost single-handedly saved a Republic communications facility.

UTILITY POUCH

Durable grip-sole boots

Obi-Wan Kenobi

IMPERTURBABLE IN BATTLE, in deep space or planetside, General Obi-Wan Kenobi still prefers negotiation to conflict. The war, however, has given him a longer view of things. Where even his lightsaber technique once reflected an affinity for deflection, his style has since become bolder and more lethal. The cause, many say, is the influence of Anakin Skywalker, and indeed Obi-Wan has become Anakin's champion to those on the Council who dread the power of the Chosen One. As a result of his military successes in the Outer Rim, General Kenobi has been granted the title "Master," and named to the Council. Even so, he feels that his education in the Force is just beginning.

Spacious, pressurized cockpit module

R4-P17 received a full body at the start of the war

Jedi/Bendu-inspired emblem, symbol of the Republic

JEDI INTERCEPTOR

Obi-Wan hates piloting, and has scant regard for astromech or other droids. Yet, he remains Anakin's steadfast wingmate in battle, trusting Anakin to pull them through tricky situations. Just as Anakin has learned patience from Obi-Wan, Obi-Wan has been spurred on to take risks.

Return Bout

Wingtip to wingtip flying is only one aspect of Obi-Wan and Anakin's friendship and mutual trust. They attack Count Dooku in concert aboard the Separatist command cruiser, lulling him into a false sense of confidence by using standard lightsaber tactics, only to shift to advanced forms, forcing a confused Dooku to retreat.

Despite his failure to take Dooku into captivity, Obi-Wan is held in great esteem by the members of the Jedi Council, who conclude that Obi-Wan is the only person skilled enough to capture the elusive and dangerous General Grievous on Utapau.

Rangefinder lock

Cushioned eyecup

JEDI MACROBINOCULARS

Projection platform

Duranium cinch-locks

SEPARATIST BINDERS

Can be uncoupled by the Force

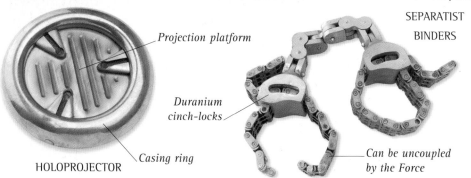

Casing ring

HOLOPROJECTOR

Leaving Anakin to face the hordes of media correspondents that flock to the flagship's crash site, Obi-Wan confers with Yoda regarding their fears that the Sith have been controlling the war from the beginning, and that Darth Sidious himself may be someone close to the Supreme Chancellor.

Powerful tail,
10 meters
(33 feet) long

Spines for defense

Crest present in
both male and
female

Five-clawed
feet provide
excellent
purchase

Unusually grave
expression

Robe is Obi-Wan's
sixth since start
of war

BOGA

On Utapau, Obi-Wan selects a
varactyl that he senses has
a constant commitment
to obedience and care for her rider.
Boga clambers to the tenth level of
Pau City with a swiftness that surprises
even Obi-Wan, only to fall later in
a hail of blaster fire unleashed by
turncoat Clone Troopers.

Compressed-air
tank

REBREATHER

The A99 Aquata Breather
Obi-Wan had used on Naboo
13 years earlier serves him all
the more on Utapau.

Obi-Wan knows that Anakin pines for
Senator Padmé Amidala. Throughout the
war, Obi-Wan has watched Anakin grow
more powerful, willful, and conflicted.

Jedi Tradition

Honoring the wishes of his former
Master, Qui-Gon Jinn, Obi-Wan has
made Anakin his life's focus, and has
instilled in Anakin his belief that the
dark side can be defeated and the
Force brought back into balance.
Yet Obi-Wan worries about
Anakin's refusal to surrender
the past, especially his fixation
with his mother's death.

Security recordings
are stored in the
Jedi Temple
data room

Obi-Wan's worst fears for Anakin are
realized when a Jedi Temple security
recording proves that Anakin has
turned to the dark side, pledged
himself to the Sith, and has
been responsible for the
murder of many Jedi
Knights and
younglings.

Fabric looks
heavier than it is

Traditional
blue blade

DATA FILE

◆ Shortly before the end of the war,
Obi-Wan and Anakin attempt but fail to
capture Dooku's dark-side apprentice,
Asajj Ventress, who remains at large.

◆ Partnered with Obi-Wan during most
of the war, R4-P17 is destroyed by buzz
droids during the Battle of Coruscant.

Jedi Knight

Niman stance, with blade cocked high

OBI-WAN SHARES Anakin's eagerness to confront Count Dooku and repay him in kind for the defeat they suffered on Geonosis. As a Jedi, though, Obi-Wan refuses to let his emotions cloud his better judgment, and fixes his attention on Supreme Chancellor Palpatine. "Rescue not mayhem," he counsels Anakin. Rendered unconscious during the duel, Obi-Wan does not witness the Count's death. However, he persuades himself that his willful former Padawan was forced to act in self-defense and has not skirted close to what the Jedi consider the dark side of the Force. Obi-Wan suspects that Palpatine has convinced Anakin that anything which is possible must be allowed.

The fight between Obi-Wan and Anakin leads to the collapse of Mustafar's shields

Utility belt houses pouches for rebreather, comlink, and liquid-cable launcher

Obi-Wan and Anakin have been partnered for so long that they can all but read each other's minds and predict what each other will do.

Swordmaster

Though a master of the Jedi lightsaber style known as Ataru, in which deflection is prized above aggression, Obi-Wan's true style is Soresu, which encourages a practitioner to place himself at the eye of the storm. Soresu is well served by Obi-Wan's innate capacity for patience and perception, but the key to mastery is audacity, a talent he has learned from Anakin.

In Anakin's flair for the dramatic and his disregard for the rules, Obi-Wan finds troubling echoes of Qui-Gon Jinn. Although Obi-Wan's student, Anakin helped mold his Master into the great Jedi Qui-Gon always thought Obi-Wan might be. This is ironic when Kenobi is forced to fight his own apprentice whom Qui-Gon ordered to be trained in the Jedi arts.

Power cell reserve cap

Ridged handgrip

OBI-WAN'S LIGHTSABER
Though it often slips from his grip, Obi-Wan's lightsaber will remain in his possession for his 19 years of self-exile on Tatooine, watching over young Luke Skywalker.

DATA FILE

◆ Obi-Wan is not without his secrets, including a relationship with Jedi Siri Tachi, who died saving Padmé.

◆ Obi-Wan is mystified by Anakin's attachment to R2-D2, and even more by the astromech's apparent attachment to Anakin.

Leading foot is firmly planted

Count Dooku

Signature look of superiority

Costly hand-woven tunic was made on Vjun

THE TITLE OF COUNT has no real meaning to Dooku, the former Jedi. It is simply the name of the political leader of the Confederacy of Independent Systems, which itself is nothing more than a fabrication, conceived by Darth Sidious as part of his plan to topple the Jedi Order and reinstate the Sith. For more than a decade now, "Dooku" has thought of himself as Darth Tyranus, apprentice to Sidious and destined to sit at his left hand as joint master of the galaxy.

A shackled Palpatine watches Dooku and Anakin duel aboard the Separatist flagship. In fact, the abduction is an elaborate ruse, engineered to ensnare Anakin and test him to determine whether he can be turned to the dark side.

Dooku's Jedi and Sith pasts meet as Anakin scissors two lightsabers at his neck. Too late, Dooku realizes Anakin is more powerful than he could have imagined.

Blade-emitter guard

Magnetic adhesion plate

DOOKU'S LIGHTSABER

Easily Replaceable

Sidious had promised to intervene in the duel, in the unlikely event that Anakin gained the upper hand. But intervention, too, was never part of the real plan. Blinded by pride, Dooku has failed to grasp that, like Darth Maul before him, he is little more than a placeholder for the apprentice Sidious has sought from the beginning: Skywalker himself.

DATA FILE

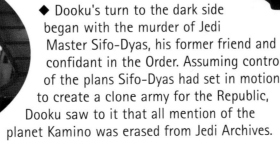

◆ Dooku's turn to the dark side began with the murder of Jedi Master Sifo-Dyas, his former friend and confidant in the Order. Assuming control of the plans Sifo-Dyas had set in motion to create a clone army for the Republic, Dooku saw to it that all mention of the planet Kamino was erased from Jedi Archives.

Dress boots of rare rancor leather

Separatist Droids

IN THEIR MANAGEMENT of the war, Darth Sidious and Count Dooku carefully ensure parity between the Republic and the Separatists. By preventing either side from attaining firepower superiority, the Sith Lords protract the war just long enough to suit their ultimate goal—the restoration of the Sith Order. Further depleting the coffers of the Trade Federation, the Sith Lords order the production of new ordnance to counter the Republic's latest generation of nimble starfighters. Fearsome, fast, and highly maneuverable, the new breed of Separatist droids threatens the most skilled clone or Jedi pilot.

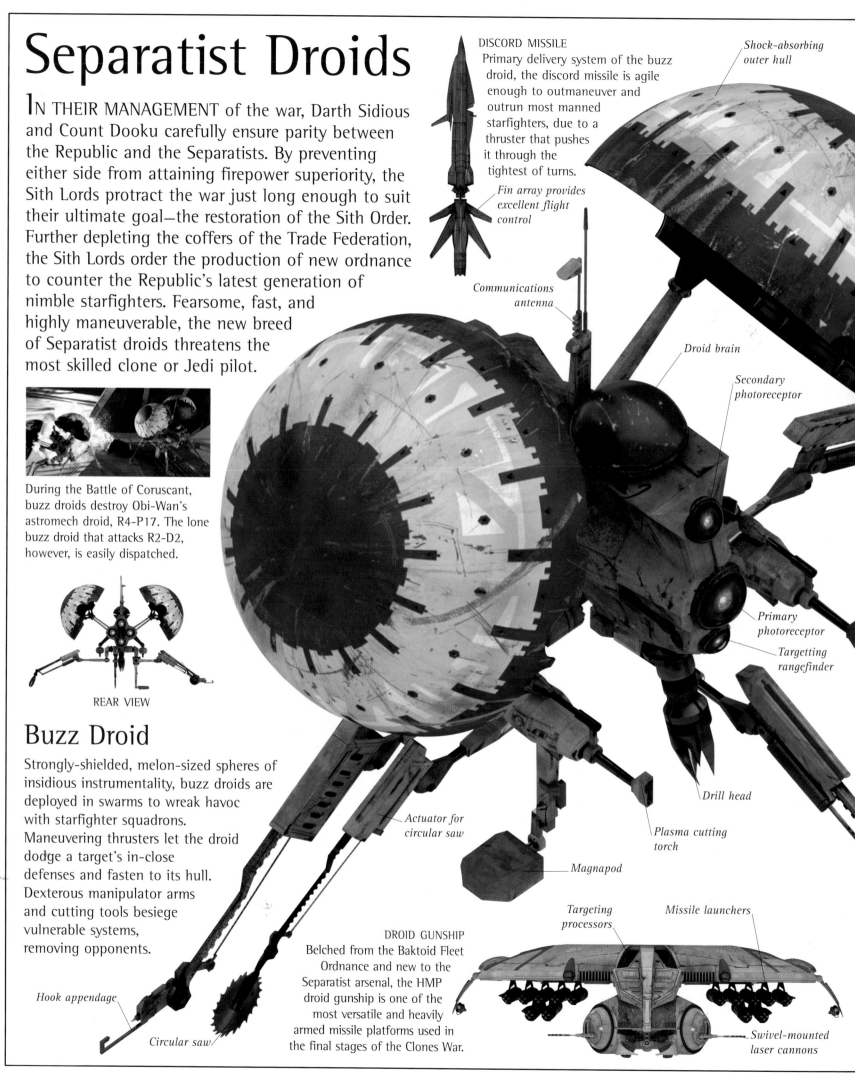

During the Battle of Coruscant, buzz droids destroy Obi-Wan's astromech droid, R4-P17. The lone buzz droid that attacks R2-D2, however, is easily dispatched.

REAR VIEW

DISCORD MISSILE
Primary delivery system of the buzz droid, the discord missile is agile enough to outmaneuver and outrun most manned starfighters, due to a thruster that pushes it through the tightest of turns.

Fin array provides excellent flight control

Shock-absorbing outer hull

Communications antenna

Droid brain

Secondary photoreceptor

Primary photoreceptor

Targetting rangefinder

Drill head

Plasma cutting torch

Magnapod

Buzz Droid

Strongly-shielded, melon-sized spheres of insidious instrumentality, buzz droids are deployed in swarms to wreak havoc with starfighter squadrons. Maneuvering thrusters let the droid dodge a target's in-close defenses and fasten to its hull. Dexterous manipulator arms and cutting tools besiege vulnerable systems, removing opponents.

Actuator for circular saw

Hook appendage

Circular saw

DROID GUNSHIP
Belched from the Baktoid Fleet Ordnance and new to the Separatist arsenal, the HMP droid gunship is one of the most versatile and heavily armed missile platforms used in the final stages of the Clones War.

Targeting processors

Missile launchers

Swivel-mounted laser cannons

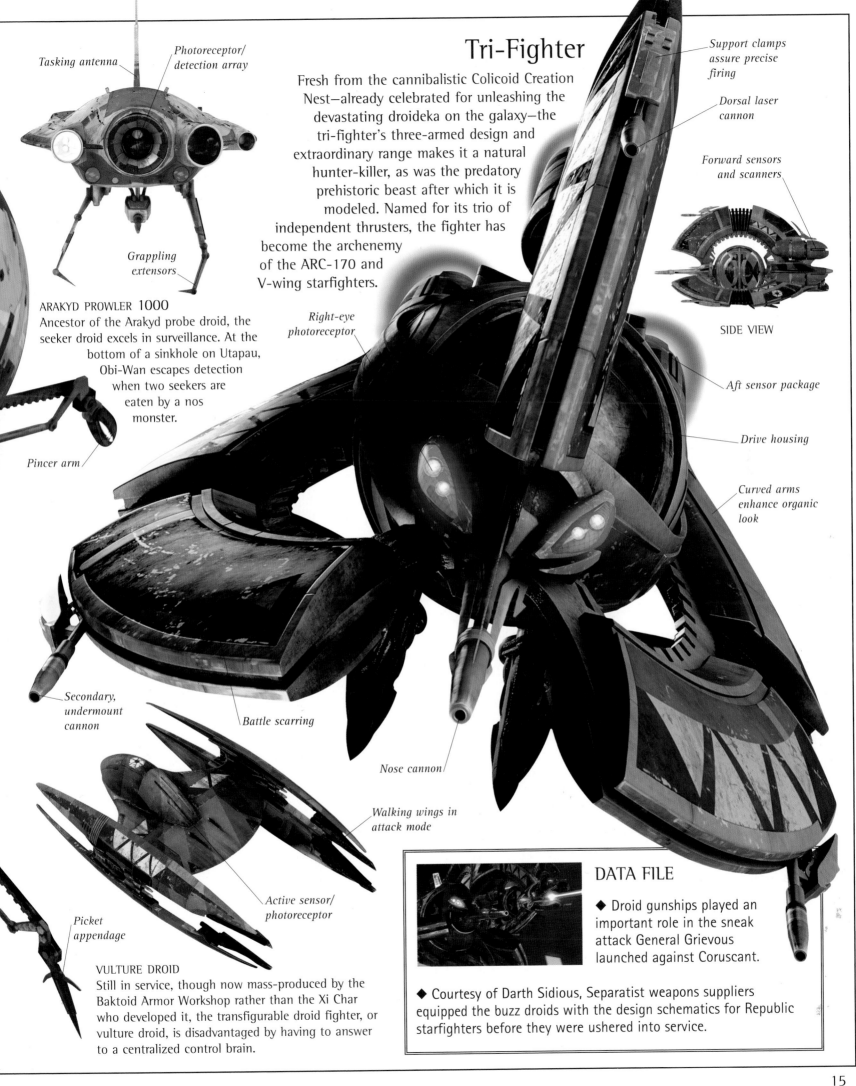

Tri-Fighter

Fresh from the cannibalistic Colicoid Creation Nest—already celebrated for unleashing the devastating droideka on the galaxy—the tri-fighter's three-armed design and extraordinary range makes it a natural hunter-killer, as was the predatory prehistoric beast after which it is modeled. Named for its trio of independent thrusters, the fighter has become the archenemy of the ARC-170 and V-wing starfighters.

Tasking antenna

Photoreceptor/ detection array

Grappling extensors

Support clamps assure precise firing

Dorsal laser cannon

Forward sensors and scanners

SIDE VIEW

ARAKYD PROWLER 1000
Ancestor of the Arakyd probe droid, the seeker droid excels in surveillance. At the bottom of a sinkhole on Utapau, Obi-Wan escapes detection when two seekers are eaten by a nos monster.

Pincer arm

Right-eye photoreceptor

Aft sensor package

Drive housing

Curved arms enhance organic look

Secondary, undermount cannon

Battle scarring

Nose cannon

Walking wings in attack mode

Active sensor/ photoreceptor

Picket appendage

VULTURE DROID
Still in service, though now mass-produced by the Baktoid Armor Workshop rather than the Xi Char who developed it, the transfigurable droid fighter, or vulture droid, is disadvantaged by having to answer to a centralized control brain.

DATA FILE

◆ Droid gunships played an important role in the sneak attack General Grievous launched against Coruscant.

◆ Courtesy of Darth Sidious, Separatist weapons suppliers equipped the buzz droids with the design schematics for Republic starfighters before they were ushered into service.

Separatist Ground Forces

THE SUPPLIERS OF SEPARATIST war machines have a long history of manufacturing droids to suit a wide range of uses and environments. The fearsome appearance of the military droids owes much to the fact that the insectoid species involved in the design phase use themselves as models. Faced with glowing photoreceptors that resemble eyes, stabilizers that mimic claws, and laser cannons that might be appendages, the soldiers of the Republic's non-clone ground forces almost forget that they are battling droids, and not living creatures.

BATTLE DROIDS
Mainstay of the Separatist infantry, battle droids are churned out on Techno Union foundry worlds. They answer to central computers, but words confuse them as much as bolts and lightsabers destroy them.

DROIDEKAS
One of the most feared armaments of the Separatist's surface arsenal, the droideka, or destroyer droid, is a self-shielded annihilator, able to deliver devastating packets of raw firepower. Droidekas help capture Obi-Wan and Anakin during their flight from the General's Quarters on Grievous's flagship, with a rescued Palpatine.

Pincer heat exhaust

Armorplast shielding

Reinforced alloy lifting rods

Communication/ sensor stalks

Blast shielding safeguards droid brain

Sensor bulb

Secondary photoreceptor

Targetting rangefinder

Twin blasters

Pressurized bolt

Pincers powered by proprietary motors

Lateral stabilizer

Prongs extend for added purchase

Crab Droid

Known to clone troopers as "The Muckracker," the crab droid is deployed on marshy worlds, such as Utapau. Heavily armored and ranging from surveillance drones that are one meter (three feet) tall to trailblazers that are six meters (twenty feet) tall, the droid can scuttle through muck to create tracks for infantry. Its front pincers also serve as vacuums, slurping up and spewing out lake-bed mud.

Duranium stabilizer can plunge into bedrock

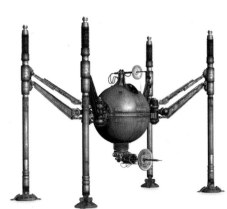

HOMING SPIDER DROID
The Commerce Guild's contribution to the ground war is the homing spider droid. It is an all-terrain weapon capable of precise targeting and sustained beam fire from its laser cannons. With surface-to-air and surface-to-surface abilities, it is a danger to Republic walkers and gunships.

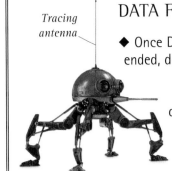
Hoop drive wheel

Hoop driver

Racks of heat-seeking missiles

Sequenced magpulse drive

Archduke Poggle the Lesser's super battle droid resembles a carapaced beetle, reared up on hind legs. Little more than an infantry droid in a durable shell, the improved model is single-minded about the task of killing.

HAILFIRE DROID
Once used by the InterGalactic Banking Clan for debt collection, the missile platform is a central component of the Separatists' rapid-deployment force. Retired from the battlefield due to its limited supply of 30 warheads, the swift, self-aware hailfire was later partnered with an air-mobile refresh droid, and regained its reputation for being the scourge of slow-moving targets.

NR-N99 Tank Droid

Once employed to persuade corporations of the wisdom of being acquired by the Corporate Alliance, the tank droid quickly became a staple in the Clone Wars, and was deployed to the Separatists' advantage on Geonosis, Kashyyyk, Cato Neimoidia, and many other worlds. An amphibious war machine, the tank can race across flat ground or shallow lakes. The circular-bodied automatons utilized early in the war were replaced by droid-piloted models, featuring superior firepower and targeting. Its treads provide amazing traction, and its side platforms are running boards for infantry droids.

Communications antenna

Tracking transmitter

Stereoscopic sensor

Drive axis hub

Primary drive tread

Modular ion cannon

Heat exchangers

Weapons outrigger

Pontoon tread

Laser cannon

R2-D2

A QUIRKY, ONE-IN-A-MILLION DROID, R2-D2 has come a long way since serving as a utility droid aboard Queen Amidala's royal starship. Time and again, the astromech has exceeded his programming, not only in the socket of a Jedi starfighter but on scores of occasions on as many worlds. He seems to delight in belittling his officious protocol counterparts, and is so perfectly attuned to Anakin's fighting spirit he may as well have been custom-built for him.

Stubborn and courageous, loyal and self-sacrificing, R2-D2 has displayed remarkable determination to succeed, despite the odds or his agile ability to calculate them.

As battle-scarred as any droid of the Republic fleet, R2-D2 provides Anakin's Jedi Interceptor with updates on ship's status, navigation, and battle assessment. The droid with a mind of his own always carries out his tasks, yet considers starfighter duty a ho-hum day job.

ARTFUL DODGER
As cunning as an intelligence operative, R2-D2 can blend in with his surroundings. Thus, he is often overlooked when super battle droids search for enemies, or starship captains memory-wipe their droids. Many underestimate R2-D2's retention powers, which will one day amaze the galaxy.

Multi-Taskmaster

Originally, only R2-D2's colors distinguished him from other astromechs. Now, courtesy of his new owner, he hosts a variety of attachments and modifications. Anakin has tweaked the droid's processor and memory matrices, and improved his interchangeable component design by upgrading his tool kit. As a result, R2-D2 can render rapid analyses of computer and starfighter weapons systems.

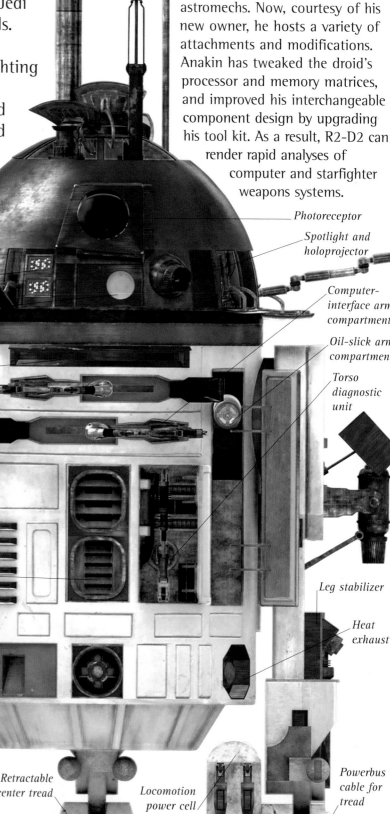

Periscope

Electric prod

Clasper arm

Photoreceptor

Spotlight and holoprojector

Computer interface arm

Logic function display

Status display

Head rotation ring

Data card input

Manipulator arms compartment

Attitude jet

Power recharge coupler

Polarity sink

Computer-interface arm compartment

Oil-slick arm compartment

Torso diagnostic unit

Leg stabilizer

Heat exhaust

Retractable center tread

Locomotion power cell

Powerbus cable for tread

R4-G9

On Utapau, Obi-Wan relies on the astromech droid R4-G9 to trick the MagnaGuards into thinking that he is departing. The droid pilots the ship away, while Obi-Wan fades into the shadows.

Recharge power coupling

Head-to-head with a super battle droid in the Federation cruiser hangar, R2-D2 does not even flinch. Although outnumbered, his use of droid bath oil will win the day.

R2-D2 can create diversions when necessary. Held aboard the flagship's bridge, he activates his loudest and most colorful systems to create a pyrotechnic display that lets Obi-Wan recall his lightsaber.

Bothersome to many, R2-D2's whistles, shrieks, and twitterings are understood by Anakin, though he relies on his viewpad display screen for translations of the astromech's sound effects.

R2-D2's bickering relationship with C-3PO changes aboard Bail Organa's starship, after C-3PO's memory is wiped to ensure the safety of Padmé's baby twins.

DATA FILE

◆ R2-D2's talent for never revealing more than he has to may be due to Anakin's modifications.

◆ After his memory wipe, C-3PO believes that he first worked with binary load-lifter droids.

A Beautiful Friendship

For R2-D2 and C-3PO, what began as a chance meeting on Tatooine will become an extended partnership, in service to Alderaanian starship captain, Raymus Antilles, and to Princess Leia Organa. Their daring exploits will become legendary, and take them across the galaxy. But only R2-D2 will have full access to their saddest memories.

Bronzium finish polished to a dazzling sheen

Audio sensor

Olfactory sensor

Supreme Chancellor Palpatine

UNFLINCHING IN HIS ASSERTION that a Republic divided against itself cannot stand, Palpatine has devoted almost half of his unprecedented 13 years in office to vanquishing the Separatist threat. Gracious and unassuming before the outbreak of the Clone Wars, he has since become Democracy's fierce champion, sacrificing his private life to assume the burden of leading the Republic to victory, the Jedi at his right hand, the Grand Army of the Republic at his left. Determined to preserve the Constitution at all costs, he is quick to maintain that he will gladly relinquish the extraordinary powers the Senate has seen fit to cede him, once the Separatists have been eliminated.

Hair is always immaculately arranged

Expression promises safety, security, justice, and peace

Senatorial collar

Cummerbund of high office

The General's Quarters aboard *Invisible Hand* bear an eerie similarity to Palpatine's chambers in the Senate Office Building. When Anakin and Obi-Wan arrive, Count Dooku is there to welcome them. Neither Jedi realizes that Dooku and Palpatine are not enemies to each other, but confederates.

Aboard Grievous's devastated flagship, Palpatine shows remarkable strength and dexterity by negotiating a precarious elevator shaft and corridors turned topsy-turvy by ruined gravity projectors.

Beneath the Mask

To some, Palpatine's guileless smile belies the visage of a shadowy, self-serving politician. Isolated by a covey of advisors, he is frequently at odds with the Jedi Council regarding the course of the war. Adept at manipulating public opinion, he buoys the Republic with carefully controlled HoloNet reports. Bent on executing a hidden agenda, he uses the war to place himself in a position where his word is law.

DATA FILE

◆ Records of Palpatine's ancestry, immediate family members, and upbringing on Naboo have mysteriously vanished.

◆ Captain Panaka, former Head of Security for Queen Amidala, gave Palpatine information regarding Anakin and Padmé's secret marriage.

Ancient demagogue, Sistros

Lethorns have thickened over the years

Speaker's staff

Chagrian cowl

Umbarans conceal their emotions

Palpatine has counseled Anakin in worldly matters, and listened to his dark confessions regarding his anger, his infatuation with Padmé, his frustrations with the Jedi Council, and even his slaughter of a tribe of Sand People on Tatooine. Their almost familial relationship is a cause of great concern to the Council.

Secret Fraternity

Senate Speaker, Mas Amedda, and Aide to the Chancellor, Sly Moore, are two among a select few who understand that Palpatine is more than he appears and that the Chancellor's look of practiced humility belies that of a cunning manipulator of political power. Palpatine's duplicity could ultimately cost them their positions—and their lives.

SLY MOORE

Force pike

Contents unknown

SITH CHALICE

Palpatine declares the Republic an Empire and himself Emperor following the defeat of the Jedi responsible for the hideous change in his appearance.

IMPERIAL GUARD
With the creation of the Empire, the Red Guard becomes the Imperial Guard. Palpatine picked its members from non-clone military units.

Shadowcloak of the Ghost Nebula

MAS AMEDDA

Though his face is irreparably damaged, Palpatine's integrity and resolve are intact and he becomes authority personified. Safety, Security, Justice, and Peace are the bywords of the New Order.

General Grievous

The blade of Jedi Master Puroth

UNKNOWN TO THE JEDI until he battled them on the Separatist foundry world of Hypori, General Grievous was actually present at the Battle of Geonosis. The carnage for which he was responsible, however, was confined to the catacombs that undermined Archduke Poggle the Lesser's Stalgasin hive complex. Named Supreme Commander of the Droid Armies in the wake of Geonosis, Grievous brought new levels of butchery to the war, laying waste to entire worlds and populations, and leaving trails of blood wherever he ventured in the Outer or Mid Rims. Although he is a cyborg, Grievous does not consider himself a droid, and reacts savagely to any such inference—as his victims would attest.

Abetted by Darths Sidious and Tyranus, Grievous carried out the long-planned abduction of Palpatine from the Chancellor's bunker on Coruscant. Unaware that he is serving both Sidious and Palpatine, Grievous does not understand why he cannot assassinate Palpatine.

DATA FILE

◆ Grievous can dislocate his shoulders and split his two arms into four.

◆ The General is secretly humiliated at having been resurrected as a cyborg.

Duranium head

Phrik alloy

Impact-driven release

High output magazine

BLASTECH CUSTOM
DT-57 "ANNIHILATOR"

Weapons of War

The uniwheel chariot Grievous pilots on Utapau is outfitted with a variety of weapons, including a powerful blaster, an energy staff of the sort wielded by his elite MagnaGuards, and a grappling hook, similar to the one he used at Coruscant to haul himself to freedom along the hull of his crippled flagship.

Retracted claws

Power-assisted shaft

GRAPPLING HOOK

Palpatine lures Obi-Wan to Separatist-occupied Utapau. With Kenobi thus occupied, Anakin has no one to guide him and is more likely to listen to the dark side.

Electromagnetic pulse generator

ENERGY STAFF

Weapons pack

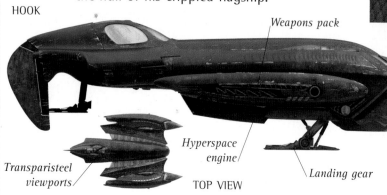

Transparisteel viewports

Hyperspace engine

Landing gear

TOP VIEW

FIGHTER

Escaping from Utapau, Obi-Wan learns that Grievous's starfighter is hyperspace-capable. After the clone trooper attack, he transmits a 9-13 Jedi emergency code over the HoloNet repeater.

Original mask carved from Mumuu skull

Sallow reptilian eyes

Engraved lines simulate original mask's karabba-blood war paint

Ultrasonic vocabulator

Grievous's hatred of the Jedi goes back to his former life as a Kaleesh warlord. Grievous captured his first lightsaber from a Jedi he defeated, and his collection has expanded ever since.

Electro-driven arms can split in half

Reinforced knee plates

Leg drivers house crystal circuitry

Upgraded LX-44 legs

Alien Warlord

Grievous's reputation as a warlord was forged during a brutal war between the Kaleesh and the Huk species. On the brink of death following a shuttle crash, Grievous was rebuilt. Neither Force-sensitive nor a Sith, the cyborg general was trained in lightsaber combat by Darth Tyranus, and is more than a match for most Jedi.

Cape contains sheath pockets for lightsabers

Powerful magnetized talons

23

Alien Cyborg

EVER ON THE ALERT for minions, Darth Sidious himself took an early interest in Kaleesh warlord Grievous. That interest continued through Grievous's reconstruction by Geonosian biotechs after his shuttle crash, with Sidious dispatching medical droids to participate in the surgical and cybernetic procedures. In the end, only Grievous's brain, spinal cord, and internal organs were transferred to the armor that would contain him as a cyborg.

Areas responsible for body coordination have been upgraded

Heuristic combat programming aids in Jedi arts training

Areas related to anger have been tampered with and areas responsible for memory have been altered

Interior of bleached armorplast death mask lined with pin-point electrodes

Grievous's own eyes enhanced with cybernetic implants

It was rumored that the shuttle crash in which the warlord nearly died had been arranged by Darth Tyranus.

Duranium teeth mimic those of Kalee's karabbac beast

Peripheral processors control speed and intensity of arm attacks

Duranium chest plates protect vulnerable gutsack

Gut sack is pressurized synthskin, allowing Grievous to survive in a vacuum

Ultrasonic vocabulator

Six-finger hands have two opposable thumbs

Trade Federation

GRIEVOUS'S FLAGSHIP, *Invisible Hand*, is a Trade Federation cruiser, originally intended for Neimoidian viceroy Nute Gunray and his advisors. Because Darth Tyranus had ordered the Neimoidians to surrender to Grievous exclusive control of their battle droid army, Gunray protested the reassignment of his personal cruiser, but his objections fell on deaf ears. As a consolation, Tyranus allowed Gunray to assign Neimoidian navigators and gunnery officers to the bridge crew.

Subordinate's miter

Mottled skin is sign of extreme stress

Tight-lipped expression of wariness

Half-closed eyes

Wave pattern weaved on mantle

Sumptuous brocaded robe

Grievous might have killed Gunray had Tyranus not intervened, warning the General that Sidious was determined to keep the Trade Federation under the Separatist umbrella.

DATA FILE

◆ On Geonosis, Gunray was not aware that Sidious was the real power behind the Confederacy of Independent Systems.

◆ The linear design of *Invisible Hand* was intended to compensate for defense weaknesses inherent in the Lucrehulk ring carriers.

Nute Gunray

The relationship between Viceroy Gunray and General Grievous got off to a rocky start when the two were first introduced on Geonosis by Count Dooku. Used to thinking of droids as utterly disposable, Gunray made the mistake of treating Grievous as just another in a long line of officer drones.

MagnaGuards

STRIDING DEFIANTLY across the surface-ravaged Huk worlds, Kaleesh warlord General Grievous was always accompanied by an elite group of warriors and bodyguards. Rebuilt as Supreme Commander of the Separatist army, he has to content himself with the Trade Federation's battle droids, which answer to a central control computer and are incapable of learning from their mistakes. Apprised of Grievous's disdain for these droids, Darth Tyranus authorizes Holowan Mechanicals to manufacture the Prototype Self-Motivating Heuristically Programmed Combat Droid, or IG-series 100 MagnaGuard, built to Grievous's specifications and trained by him.

The MagnaGuards score a victory on *Invisible Hand*, taking Anakin, Obi-Wan, and Supreme Chancellor Palpatine into custody after the trio are trapped in a ray-shielded stretch of corridor. But General Grievous's gloating is short-lived, however, after a diversionary move by R2-D2 sends the bridge into chaos.

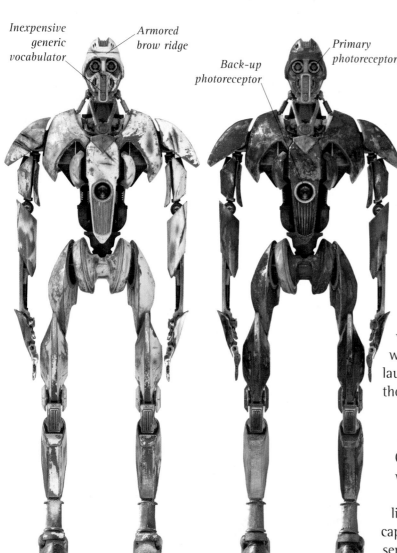

Inexpensive generic vocabulator

Armored brow ridge

Back-up photoreceptor

Primary photoreceptor

Discharge capacitor

Power cycling coil

Power cell

EMP field generator

Focusing rods

When the smoke clears, the MagnaGuards are in pieces. The remainder of Grievous's elite will suffer a similar fate on Utapau, in a warm-up round for Obi-Wan's match with the cyborg commander.

Model Guards

Holowan Mechanicals made several MagnaGuard models, distinguished by color: black, alabaster, blue, and the rare gray. Each two-meter (6.5-ft) tall droid specializes in a form of combat, and is equipped with an electrostaff or dedicated weapons, from grenades to rocket launchers. Headclothes pay tribute to those worn by Grievous's original elite.

Electrostaffs

Constructed of costly phrik alloy and equipped with electromagnetic pulse-generating tips, the MagnaGuards electrostaffs are resistant to lightsaber strikes. While certain types of staff are capable of neutralizing ray shields, the standard staff serves primarily as a melee weapon, meting out fatal blunt-force injuries in the hands of its wielders.

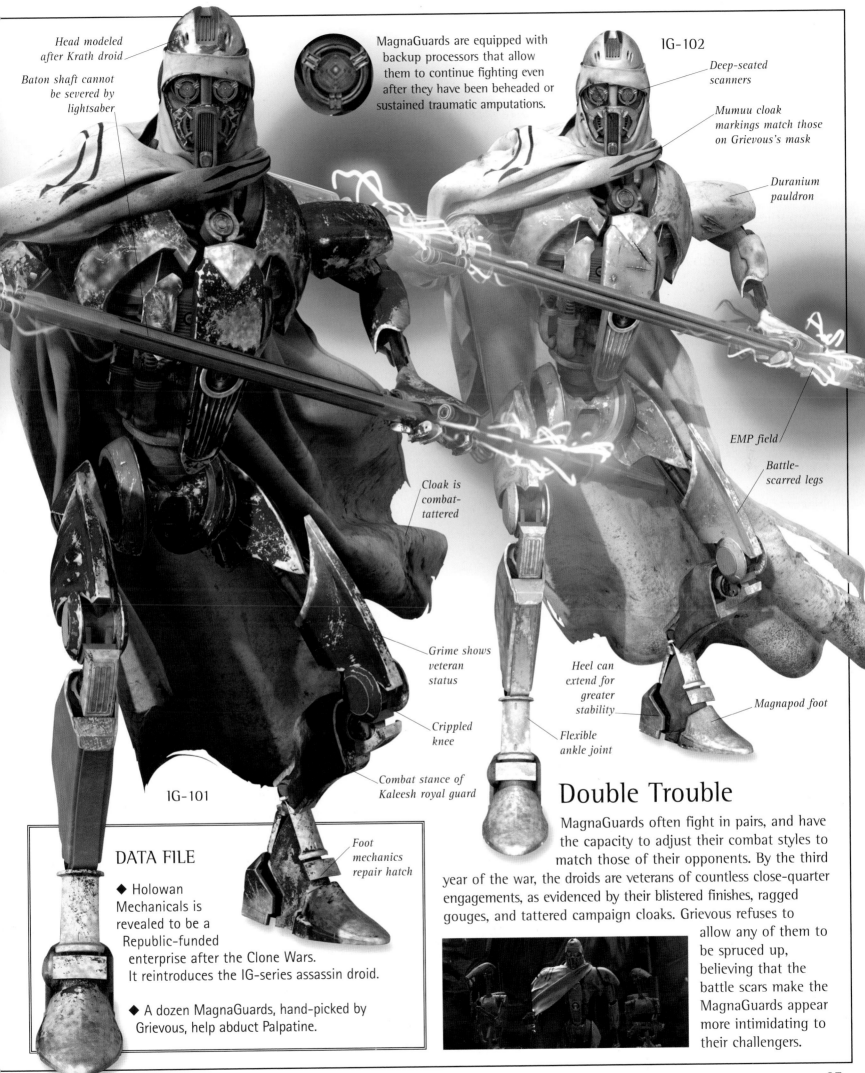

Head modeled
after Krath droid

Baton shaft cannot
be severed by
lightsaber

MagnaGuards are equipped with
backup processors that allow
them to continue fighting even
after they have been beheaded or
sustained traumatic amputations.

IG-102

Deep-seated
scanners

Mumuu cloak
markings match those
on Grievous's mask

Duranium
pauldron

Cloak is
combat-
tattered

EMP field

Battle-
scarred legs

Grime shows
veteran
status

Crippled
knee

Combat stance of
Kaleesh royal guard

IG-101

Heel can
extend for
greater
stability

Flexible
ankle joint

Magnapod foot

Double Trouble

MagnaGuards often fight in pairs, and have
the capacity to adjust their combat styles to
match those of their opponents. By the third
year of the war, the droids are veterans of countless close-quarter
engagements, as evidenced by their blistered finishes, ragged
gouges, and tattered campaign cloaks. Grievous refuses to

allow any of them to
be spruced up,
believing that the
battle scars make the
MagnaGuards appear
more intimidating to
their challengers.

DATA FILE

◆ Holowan
Mechanicals is
revealed to be a
Republic-funded
enterprise after the Clone Wars.
It reintroduces the IG-series assassin droid.

◆ A dozen MagnaGuards, hand-picked by
Grievous, help abduct Palpatine.

Foot
mechanics
repair hatch

Coruscant Ground Crew

WITH TENS OF THOUSANDS of ships arriving on Coruscant at any given moment, an army of landing-platform personnel stands by to assist in off-loading, refueling, and basic maintenance. Considered by many to be work fit more for droids than flesh-and-bloods, most so-called ground crew workers are poorly educated and underpaid.

Heat-resistant faceplate

Integrated heads-up display

Blast-proof goggles

FIRE FIGHTER

Plastoid helmet contains comlink

MECHANIC

Generic utility suit

Breathmask for oxygen supply

Boot-guards impregnated with lead

Slop footwear

Emitter for flame-retardant foam

Emergency running lights

Ablative cockpit canopy

FIRE-SUPPRESSION SHIP
Two members of Fire Team Three, a daredevil burn-off brigade, died during the attempt to extinguish the flames engulfing the Separatist flagship when it plunged into Coruscant's upper atmosphere.

Annunciator and siren

TOUCHDOWN
Anakin's ability to pilot the deteriorating flagship to safety is extraordinary. To avoid adding to the massive damage Coruscant has already sustained, he guides *Invisible Hand* to a seldom-used landing platform in the industrial sector.

BACKPACK UNIT
Fire-suppression is a high-risk job. Due to the exotic nature of the fuels that power some cargo landers and shuttles, shipboard fires often become infernos, costing lives.

High-pressure emitter nozzle

Backpack is made of lightweight alloy

Heat-resistant and weatherproof housing

Discharge trigger

Fire Brigades

At the highest end of the ground-crew spectrum are the skilled workers of Coruscant's fire-fighting teams. Some are headquartered mid-level in the sheer cityscape, while others patrol the autonavigation lanes that striate the upper reaches of the galactic capital's skies.

DATA FILE

◆ After the war, many clone troopers retired from service because of battlefield injuries, innate deterioration, or accelerated aging.

◆ These troopers will be reassigned to boost landing platform-maintenance and emergency rapid-reaction squads.

Coruscant High Life

CORUSCANT SEEMS MUCH AS it was ten years earlier, before anyone considered Count Dooku's Separatist movement a threat. However, clone troopers now stand guard at landing platforms and public buildings, and new laws allow searches and seizures of private property. The war has made many Coruscanti wealthy, and Senators still enjoy the kickbacks to which they have grown accustomed.

By good fortune or design, Palpatine managed to keep the surface battle from escalating. After his abduction, however, the mood in the capital grows tense, and disquieting rumors spread.

Command cap is as phony as rank

Artificially colored lekku

WAKS TRODE

Sy Myrthian mantilla hides secret recording device

Wide-angle vision

RYSTÁLL SANT

Crime-syndicate concubine hairstyle

GREEATA   CPT. FAYTONNI   KOYI MATEIL

OPERA DRESS
Nights at the opera are occasions for revelry and excess. Many patrons wear costumes that rival those worn by the performers.

DELVA RACINE

Privileged Few

Many new restaurants and clubs have opened on Coruscant. But the elite prefer to gather at the Galaxies Opera House for performances by troupes from many star systems. Palpatine often attends, if his schedule permits, preferring Galaxies to the older opera house patronized by wealthy members of the Valorum family.

BROOKISH BOONE

DATA FILE

◆ A Mon Calamari performance is in progress when Anakin arrives at Palpatine's private box, where he is told that clone intelligence has discovered the whereabouts of Grievous.

◆ It is thought that Baron Papanoida may be a double agent.

Padmé Amidala

TIME AND AGAIN Padmé has found herself at the center of galactic events. Her illegal presence on Geonosis to effect the rescue of Obi-Wan Kenobi is seen by some as the spark that ignited the Clone Wars.

Padmé has earned a reputation for boldness, but now she is torn by choices she has made in her private life, and she sometimes dreams of retiring into seclusion on Naboo. However, her activist side is not easily suppressed.

Elaborate coiffure originated on Naboo

Heirloom suspensas

Rich cape enfolds Padmé completely

In the three years since their secret marriage on Naboo, Padmé and Anakin have found refuge in each other's embrace. But their trysts have been brief and clandestine. They haven't met in five months when Palpatine's abduction returns Anakin to Coruscant.

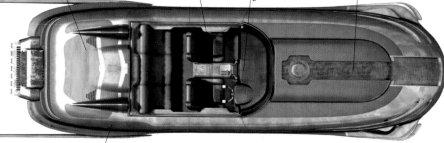

Anti-tracking device *Tractor field seats* *Secret compartment for blaster* *Souped-up engine*

Aerodynamic yet classic styling

CLASSIC SPEEDER
Padmé's classic-style speeder whisks her to and from the landing platform where her starship is berthed. Anakin has modified the speeder's engine.

Senator

Padmé's voice in the Senate is still as powerful as it was before the start of the war. While Anakin commands legions of clone troopers in the Outer Rim, Padmé and other members of the Loyalist Committee attempt to find peaceful resolution to the ongoing conflict. Yet her critics say that she has turned a blind eye to the increasingly oppressive climate on Coruscant, to the loss of rights guaranteed by the Constitution, and to the growing power of Palpatine.

DATA FILE

◆ Handmaidens Moteé and Ellé were chosen because they resemble Padmé. They know of her marriage to Anakin, and often facilitate the couple's meetings by serving as decoys.

◆ After the massacre at the Jedi Temple, the official explanation is that Padmé and many Senators had been killed by the Jedi.

Ensconced in Naboo's platform in the Senate Rotunda, Padmé witnesses the death of democracy, as Palpatine proclaims the Republic an Empire, and himself Emperor for life. The ovation he receives shows that anyone can fall victim to the machinations of an evil leader.

THE BEST OF TIMES
With its private landing platform, lofty veranda, and several entrances, Padmé's penthouse in the arch-topped summit of the Senate Apartment Complex is near perfect for rendezvous with Anakin. By Senatorial standards, the penthouse is modest in size and decor, though most Coruscanti would consider it to be flagrantly opulent.

Preoccupied expression

Harness eases back pain

Remote control receiver

WISH GLOBE

Globe creates seemingly sourceless light

ILLUMINATOR

Ancient moon goddess pose

Padmé has adorned her rooms with items from her Lake District residence.

SHIRAYA STATUE

Double Life

Like Anakin and Palpatine, Padmé is adept at hiding her true nature. But she is unable to completely conceal the facts of her pregnancy: the fullness of her figure and her frequent distraction. Senatorial scandals are nothing new, but Padmé's secret could destroy Anakin's life as a public hero, and forever foil his hopes of being named to the Jedi Council.

MUSTAFAR
Refusing to believe Obi-Wan when he says that Anakin has been turned to the dark side, Padmé races to Mustafar in her starship.

QUEEN APAILANA

Cerlin capelet

Chersilk mourning robe

Gravely injured by Anakin's Force choke, Padmé is brought to a nearby medical facility on Polis Massa. Dying, despite the care she is given, she tells Obi-Wan that she still feels there is good in Anakin.

RUWEE   SOLA   JOBAL

Boots contain cushioned inserts

Naboo Funeral

Padmé's parents Ruwee and Sola, sister Jobal, and Queen Apailana, are told that Padmé was killed by the Jedi on Coruscant. No mention is made of Padmé's pregnancy or where R2-D2 and C-3PO are. An investigation into who fathered the children would go against Naboo tradition.

The Senate

WHERE GREED AND CORRUPTION defined the pre-war Senate, dereliction of duty and indolence have been the bywords since. Reasoned discourse and spirited debate are now viewed as archaic practices, impediments to the "efficient streamlining of the bureaucratic process." In the climate of fear spawned by the war, most Senators find it easier—some say safer—to place their personal convictions on hold, and to ratify any piece of legislation that cedes greater power to Supreme Chancellor Palpatine or to any of the committees responsible for overseeing the war effort. Typically, the Senate is so busy modifying the Republic Constitution that it has completely abandoned its role as a balancing arm of the government.

Republic Senate

Executive Annex Dome

SENATE BUILDING
Rising from the center of the Legislative District, the Senate comes under attack by vulture fighters and droid gunships during General Grievous's sudden raid on Coruscant. While the building emerges unscathed, nearby edifices, landing platforms, and plazas suffer major damage. In the Nicandra Counterrevolutionary Signalmen's Memorial Building alone, fatalities number in the thousands.

FANG ZAR

Sern Prime topknot

High-status beard

Senatorial gown

Fashionable translator

TERR TANEEL

CHI EEKWAY

Molf-tasseled overcloak

Kuati turban

Formal shoulder sash

GIDDEAN DANU

Hairstyle is a plea for peace

MALÉ-DEE

Visdic body wrappings

Giddean Danu and Malé-Dee are among a group of Senators opposing Palpatine. They believe that he may respond if he is told that there are other disaffected Senators.

Noble Politicians

Palpatine and his parties of aides and red-robed guards have not cowed all the Senators. A loyal group has signed "The Petition of the Two Thousand," which states in no uncertain terms that the time has come for the Supreme Chancellor to yield some of the emergency powers that were granted him. It also demands that he open cease-fire negotiations with representatives of the Confederacy of Independent Systems.

SPY CAM

Coruscanti have demonstrated a great willingness to surrender personal freedoms in the name of safety. Even severe security measures are now accepted without question. Inside the Senate, new procedures allow for eavesdropping by hovercams.

Control antenna

Telephoto lens

Unknown to Palpatine, the two Senators most responsible for drawing up the Petition of the Two Thousand are Bail Organa, representing the Core world Alderaan, and Mon Mothma, daughter of a former governor of Chandrila. Politically savvy but very headstrong, Mon Mothma encourages Bail to draw outspoken Padmé Amidala into their confidence, convinced that Padmé's well-known loyalty to Palpatine can work to the petitioners' advantage.

Antique Chandrilan headpiece

Serene expression

Hanna pendant

Privacy screens can no longer be activated in the Senate Rotunda. Many delegates are therefore afraid to whisper their reactions, let alone speak their minds. Hovercams slink about, relaying recordings to security chief Armand Isard.

Sarrish Defense Force tunic

Calamarian collar gives moisture

Beak can crack shellfish

VEEDAAZ AWMETTH

MEENA TILLS

GUME SAAM

Large, flat teeth for methodical chewing

Costly Andalian cloak

Tube-like eye sockets give face inverted look

ASK AAK

SOLIPO YEB

SWEITT CONCORKILL

Shimmersilk mantle

Heads of State

Even before the abrupt end to the Clone Wars, many Senators representing Outer Rim worlds avoided Coruscant. They feared retribution for having forged trade agreements with species identified with the Separatist movement. By contrast, those Senators who were shrewd enough to remain on Coruscant and side with Palpatine found themselves rewarded in the post-war years.

DATA FILE

◆ Until the election of Princess Leia Organa to the Imperial Senate, Mon Mothma is the youngest Senator ever to hold office.

◆ Mon Mothma, Bail Organa, and his adopted daughter, Leia, will all play pivotal roles in the formation of the Rebel Alliance.

Cranial plates
revealed by
angry scowl

Rarely bared claws

Yoda

WHEN YODA FIRST ARRIVED at the Jedi Temple more than 800 years ago, memories of the Jedi–Sith War and the waning of the Dark Times were still fresh. Since then, this Jedi Master has witnessed the full flowering of the Jedi Order, and of the Republic itself. For the past two centuries, however, Yoda has been aware of a gradual re-emergence of the dark side. As the end of the Clone Wars draws near, he foresees that the most significant dangers to the Jedi Order have yet to be faced.

Ancient
lightsaber

Homespun robe

Accepting finally that the war has been nothing more than a manipulation by the Sith to undermine the Jedi Order, Yoda decides to act on his instincts.

Bloused
pants

*Yoda's staff is a gift
from the Wookiees*

Master

Yoda has guided hundreds of Jedi to knighthood. But some Jedi believe that he has failed to provide the Order with enlightened leadership. For these same Jedi, Yoda has placed too much trust in the prophesized ability of the Chosen One to restore balance to the Force.

Tridactyl feet
spread wide

Safe aboard the *Tantive IV*, Yoda learns of the clone trooper attack on the Jedi Temple. He concludes that Mace and the others failed to defeat Darth Sidious.

GIMER STICK

When Yoda arrives at Palpatine's holding office beneath the Senate Rotunda, he is in no mood for interference. Before the Chancellor's red guards can so much as brandish their force pikes, Yoda flattens them with a Force push.

In his contest with Sidious, Yoda realizes he is overmatched and deserts the fight, perhaps because his spirit has been broken by so many Jedi deaths. However, he remains determined to achieve victory over the dark side.

Increasingly troubled by the gathering of the dark side around the Chancellor, the Jedi Council resolve to capture General Grievous and then force Palpatine to abdicate.

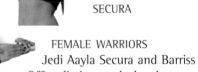

Second heart is needed to nourish large brain

Antitox breath mask

High parry stance

PLO KOON

LUMINARA UNDULI

Djem So attack stance

AAYLA SECURA

Kai-Kan drop stance

BARRISS OFFEE

FEMALE WARRIORS
Jedi Aayla Secura and Barriss Offee die in attacks by clone troopers on the murky world of Felucia. Light-years distant, Luminara Unduli is lost on the Wookiee world of Kashyyyk.

Jedi Leaders

Since Geonosis, the Jedi have led legions of clone troopers into combat on hundreds of worlds. As a result, they are spread thinly throughout the galaxy. When clone commanders receive Palpatine's traitorous Order 66, Masters, Knights, and Padawans are taken by surprise. They are assassinated by the troopers with whom they have served.

Sensor processor and guidance computer

Escape pods loft Yoda to safety from Kashyyyk, and to sanctuary on Dagobah.

On Polis Massa, late-Jedi Master, Qui-Gon Jinn, begins tutoring Yoda on how to survive death with one's consciousness intact. In time, Yoda tells Obi-Wan of this, and that he, too, will soon begin training with Qui-Gon.

KI-ADI-MUNDI

ESCAPE POD

Mace Windu

GIFTED WITH A TALENT for seeing to the very heart of a matter, Mace Windu has long nursed suspicions about Palpatine. Shortly before the Chancellor's abduction, Mace worried openly that Palpatine had fallen under the influence of the as-yet unidentified Sith Lord, Darth Sidious. But Yoda cautioned that the Senate would need proof of the Chancellor's treachery. Mace's concern blossoms into certainty when Palpatine refuses to tender a peace offer to the Separatists, even after Count Dooku has been killed.

Traditional hooded robe

Somber expression

Coarseweave tunic

After Palpatine defies tradition by appointing Anakin to the Jedi Council as his voice, Mace, Obi-Wan, and Yoda discuss the Sith threat to the Republic. They reluctantly decide to order Anakin to act as a double agent in the Chancellor's office.

Modulation circuitry for amethyst blade

Power cell

WINDU'S LIGHTSABER
Mace's lightsaber technique synthesizes deadly Form VII with a newly created form known as vaapad. A Force-user who practices this form may skirt close to the dark side.

Determined Jedi

Anakin's revelation—that Palpatine and Darth Sidious are one in the same—hollows Mace to the core. Not days earlier, he and other Jedi had risked their lives against Grievous's droid forces to prevent Palpatine from being abducted. Grasping that the abduction and the war itself has been nothing more than a deception, Mace leaps into action, promising to take Palpatine into Jedi custody, dead or alive.

DATA FILE

◆ Mace's precognitive abilities give him keen insight into individuals and events.

◆ Yoda agreed that Mace should arrest Palpatine if the Supreme Chancellor was discovered to have had dealings with Darth Sidious.

Lightsaber Masters

Most of the Jedi are deployed on distant worlds, but Mace manages to assemble a trio of celebrated swordmasters to assist him in arresting Palpatine: Agen Kolar, a Zabrak known among the Jedi to strike first and ask questions later; Saesee Tiin, a solitary Iktotchi who has never chosen a Padawan learner; and Kit Fisto, Nautolan master of Form 1 lightsaber technique, who distinguished himself on Geonosis and Mon Calamari, and who partnered Mace in battling Grievous on Coruscant.

When Anakin Skywalker was a boy, Mace came to accept he could be the Chosen One and eventually advocated that he be trained as a Jedi. A decade later, Mace has his doubts about Skywalker, and is disturbed by his relationship with Palpatine.

Entering Palpatine's quarters in the Senate Office Building, Mace doesn't fully grasp that Palpatine has been waiting a lifetime for just such a contest. Accusing the Jedi of treason, the Sith Lord conjures a lightsaber from the sleeve of his robe, and the fight is on.

Mace's Jedi team advances on Palpatine, confident that they can defeat Sidious. Allowing vaapad to flow through him, Mace leaps to engage the Sith Lord, unaware that the person who will figure most in his own death is not Sidious, but Anakin.

Horns regenerate over time

Tough skin impervious to winds of homeworld

Well-developed horns

Nautolans are amphibious

Chemically sensitive tentacles

KIT FISTO

SAESEE TIIN

Iridonian field boots

AGEN KOLAR

Deadly Confrontation

Only four Jedi of Mace's generation have fought a Sith Lord. Qui-Gon Jinn is dead; Yoda and Obi-Wan are on Kashyyyk and Utapau; and Anakin cannot be relied on, now that Sidious has tempted him with apprenticeship. Before Mace realizes what has happened, Kolar, Tiin, and Fisto have fallen to Sidious's blade.

Raised hood for stealth

Anakin—Fallen Jedi

WHILE ANAKIN SKYWALKER'S SLIDE to the dark side seems abrupt, the tragedy is rooted in his upbringing as a slave on Tatooine, and in the death of his mother, abducted and tortured by a band of Tusken Raiders. His experiences during the Clone Wars have eroded his faith in both the Jedi and the Senate, neither of which he believes capable of restoring peace and order to the galaxy. Though manipulated and exploited by Chancellor Palpatine, Anakin ultimately agrees to apprentice himself to the Sith Lord, in order to prevent Padmé Amidala from dying.

Anakin takes a significant stride toward the dark side when he kills the defeated Count Dooku aboard the Separatist flagship. Urged to greater violence by Palpatine—then forgiven by him—Anakin gives in to his rage and craving for vengeance.

The Dark Side

Blinded by fear and anger, Anakin fails to realize how easily he has played into Palpatine's hands. Anakin pledges his allegiance to the Supreme Chancellor—now revealed to be Darth Sidious—and the Sith. In so doing, he rejects his destiny as the Chosen One, and seals the fate of the Jedi order.

Anakin's frightening visions foretell Padmé's death during childbirth on a world remote from Coruscant.

While its design suggests that of a fortress, the Jedi Temple has stood as a symbol of peace and justice for more than 40 generations. But with so many Jedi deployed on far-flung worlds, the Temple is relatively unprotected.

The computer room houses controls for the Temple's network of communications systems. The Jedi beacon enables near-instantaneous contact between the Temple and Jedi in the field, without relying on the HoloNet.

Tholoth headdress

Hollow montrals sense space

STASS ALLIE

Characteristic pigmentation of the Togruta species

SHAAK TI

Dubbed Darth Vader by Sidious, Anakin embarks on a murderous rampage through the halls of the Temple that has been his home for 13 years. He and hundreds of clone troopers kill Jedi swordmaster Cin Drallig, as well as teachers, teens, and younglings.

Evidence of Anakin's slaughter bloodies the stately halls of the Temple. Administrators and students pose little threat to Palpatine's plans but Anakin does not care. Carrying out the executions is Anakin's way of swearing allegiance to the dark side and ensuring his family's survival.

Stass Allie and Shaak Ti

With almost all able-bodied Jedi Knights deployed far from Coruscant, the training of young Jedi has been cut. Those who remain in residence are left to fend for themselves. Even the Temple's finest swordmaster is no match for Anakin Skywalker and the stormtroopers of the 501st Legion. Not one Jedi knight or youngling will survive the horrific onslaught.

Sidious assures his new apprentice that the murders of those he loves will allow him to tap deeply into the powers afforded by the dark side of the Force. The Jedi must be the first to die—and that means all of them.

DATA FILE

◆ Anakin knew his atrocities were being monitored, but he was confident his actions would help him to attain a position of power where he was answerable only to Palpatine.

◆ Yoda and Obi-Wan recalibrate the beacon's Return-to-Coruscant code to save Jedi survivors.

Elite Clones

THE KAMINOANS, WHO BUILT the clone army, believed the Jedi Knights were too few in number to serve as an elite force or as field commanders for millions of soldiers. So they provided some of the clones with enhanced programming and extra training, which allowed them to function as special forces or chain-of-command links between the Jedi and standard troopers. These clones displayed initiative and leadership ability, and closely resembled their bounty hunter template.

Advanced Recon

The Kaminoans created a select number of clone troopers to be trained personally by bounty hunter Jango Fett. Designated Advanced Recon Commandos (ARCs), they worked in teams to execute special missions. Elite ARC squads were deployed soon after the war began on Muunilinst and other strategic worlds. They operated autonomously, but reported to Jedi Generals.

Clone commanders use names in addition to numerical designations. This practice was initiated by the Jedi themselves, as well as other progressive-thinking officials in the Republic, to foster a growing fellowship. Thus, CC 2224 came to be called Cody; 1004, Gree; and 1138, Bacara.

Color denotes
legion affiliation

Reinforced
tactical boots

COMMANDER
CODY

Standard-issue
DC-15A rifle

DC-15A
standard
blaster

POLARIZED
MACROBINOCULARS

Heat dispersion
vent

ARC pauldron

Spare blaster
magazines

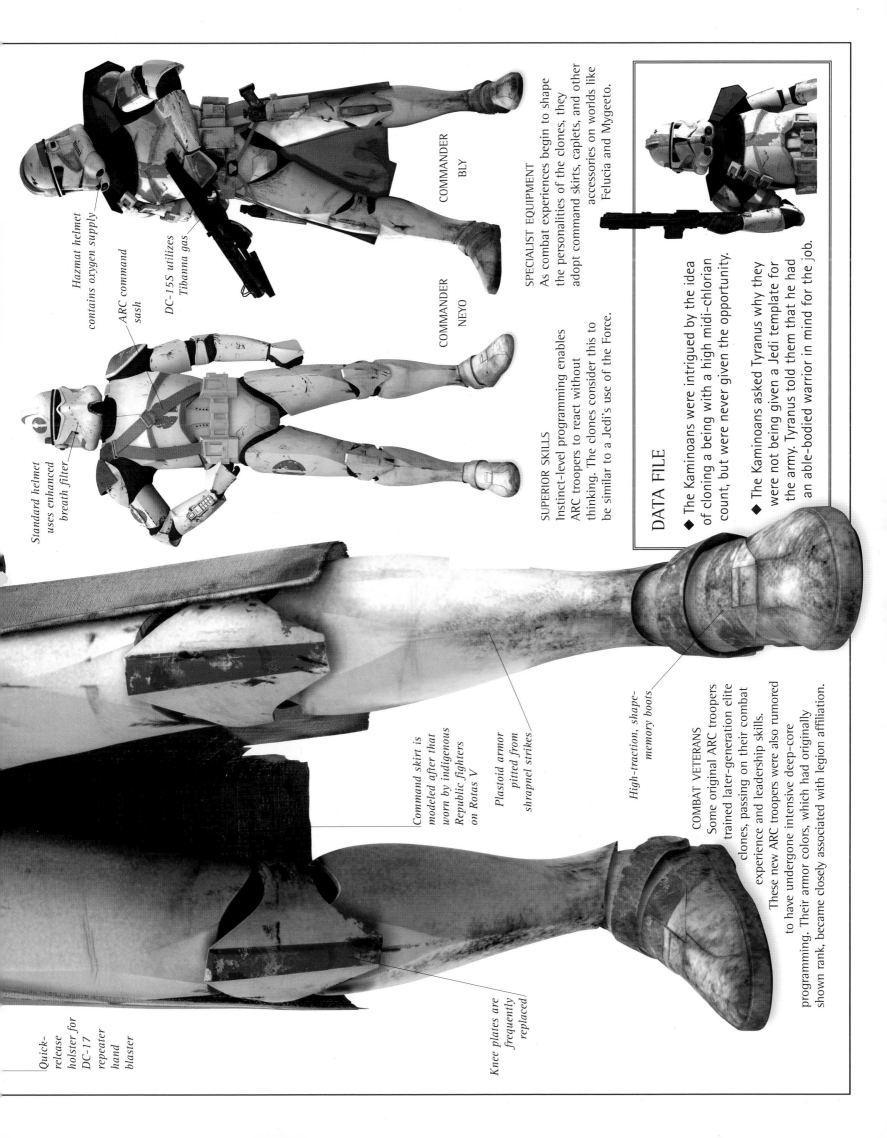

Standard helmet uses enhanced breath filter

Hazmat helmet contains oxygen supply

ARC command sash

DC-15S utilizes Tibanna gas

COMMANDER BLY

COMMANDER NEYO

SPECIALIST EQUIPMENT
As combat experiences begin to shape the personalities of the clones, they adopt command skirts, caplets, and other accessories on worlds like Felucia and Mygeeto.

SUPERIOR SKILLS
Instinct-level programming enables ARC troopers to react without thinking. The clones consider this to be similar to a Jedi's use of the Force.

DATA FILE

◆ The Kaminoans were intrigued by the idea of cloning a being with a high midi-chlorian count, but were never given the opportunity.

◆ The Kaminoans asked Tyranus why they were not being given a Jedi template for the army. Tyranus told them that he had an able-bodied warrior in mind for the job.

Quick-release holster for DC-17 repeater hand blaster

Knee plates are frequently replaced

Command skirt is modeled after that worn by indigenous Republic fighters on Rotas V

Plastoid armor pitted from shrapnel strikes

High-traction, shape-memory boots

COMBAT VETERANS
Some original ARC troopers trained later-generation elite clones, passing on their combat experience and leadership skills. These new ARC troopers were also rumored to have undergone intensive deep-core programming. Their armor colors, which had originally shown rank, became closely associated with legion affiliation.

Clone Specialists

THE GRAND ARMY'S need for specialization is not limited to the production of support droids. Select clone troopers are trained in the use of new speeder bikes, rocket packs, and all-terrain vehicles. Others are trained in long-range reconnoitering, assassination, underwater demolition, and computer slicing. Recruited from mercenary groups and crime cartels, the instructors subject the troopers to live-fire exercises in which many clones die. The results, however, are teams of combat specialists that can be deployed in a host of environments, and against rare Separatist non-droid forces.

Tinted visor reduces glare by 70%

Air-supply hose made of tempered plastoid

Front-carry forced-ox rebreather

Flight data records pouch

Flightsuit clings to kneecap armor

Thermal outer boot worn over flight slipper

Projectile cannon

Laser cannon

Split wings

ARC-170

Clone Pilot

LAAT-gunship pilots were part of the war from the start, but a new breed of pilots was required to fly the hyperspace-capable ARC-170 and V-wing starfighters. Squadron pilots trained together, receiving programming on Kamino before being sent to Coruscant system worlds for advanced schooling.

Aggressive ReConnaissance-170 starfighters led by Clone Commander Odd Ball fly with Skywalker and Kenobi during the Battle of Coruscant.

Swivel-mounted saddle and blaster

Laser cannon

Reverse-articulation coupler

POD WALKER
Descended from the All Terrain Personal Transport, the AT-AP (All Terrain Attack Pod) is armed with blaster cannons. Deployed with mechanized platoons, the scout's adjustable leg-suspension system gives stability and maneuverability.

DATA FILE

◆ Sheathed in Katarn armor and trained by Mandalorian instructors, Republic commandos operate in teams to recruit and train provincial forces, or execute sabotage missions. On Kashyyyk, the commandos of Delta Squad free Tarfful from Trandoshan captivity.

Shock Trooper

To the increasing frustration of the Jedi, Palpatine's War Council Advisory Panel, along with Senate committees under the aegis of the HomeWorld Security Command, is responsible for the deployment of clone specialists. On Coruscant, red-emblazoned shock troopers patrol public plazas and keep watch on government buildings and landing platforms. Citizens of the capital world are required to present their identity cards on demand.

Coruscant designation

Upgraded breath filter and annunciator

Powerful turbofan

Forward blasters

Terrain-laser scanner

SWAMP SPEEDER

SPEEDER TYPES
By the end of the war, several varieties of the speeder bike have been introduced, including the swamp and the BARC. Driven by a powerful turbofan, the swamp speeder can seat two clones, side-by-side.

Repulsorlift engine

BARC SPEEDER

Legion designation

Enhanced helmet comlinks

Motion detection scanner

Control yoke

Heat dissipater

In the wake of the Jedi's failed attempt to arrest Palpatine, shock troopers accompany him to the Senate. Already, a list of possibly traitorous Senators is being compiled.

Linkage

Visor adapted for greater visibility

Stock holds power-charge magazine

Shaped charges

Repeating blaster

Reverse articulated legs

AT-RT
The spry All Terrain Recon Transport is an essential element of Grand Army mechanized units and reconnaissance platoons. It is equipped with enhanced communication arrays to provide forward command bases with updated situation reports.

DC-15 rifle

Camouflage armor is developed for jungle worlds. Some clones are shocked that not all environments are as clean as Kamino.

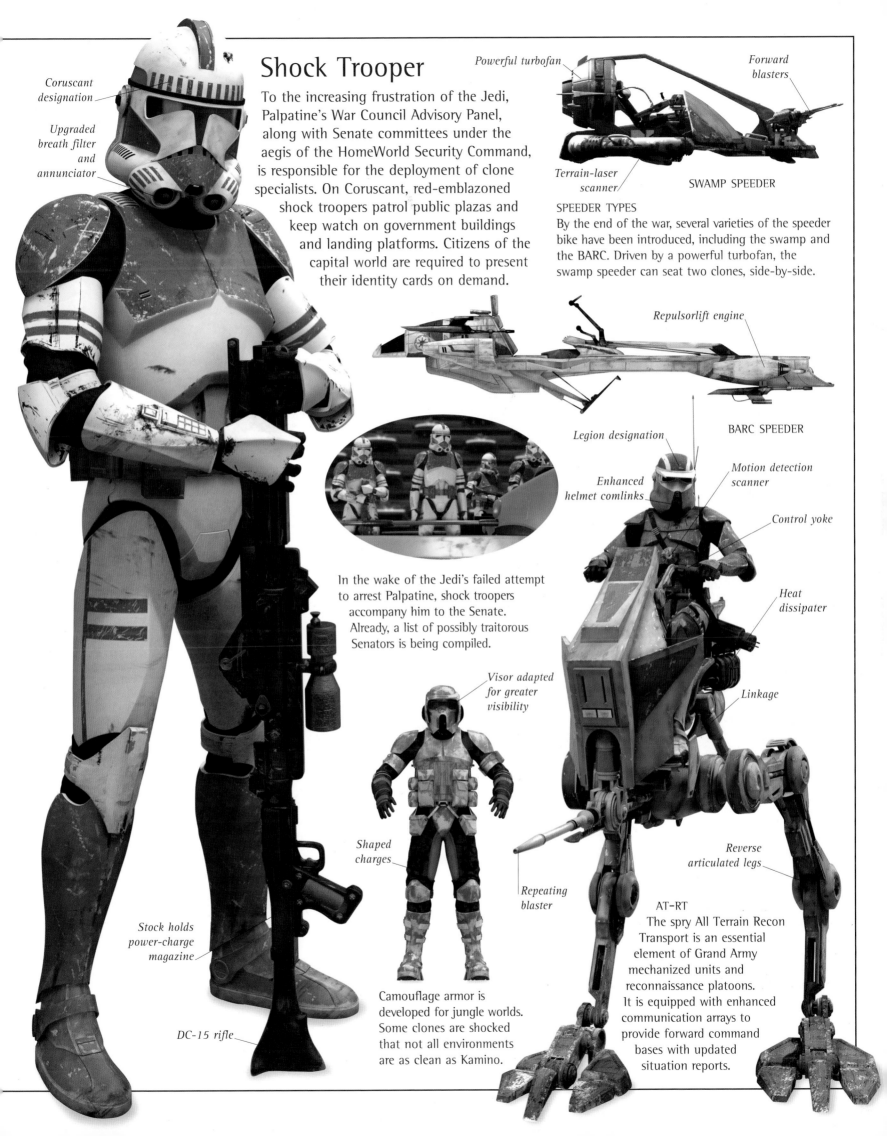

Clone Troopers

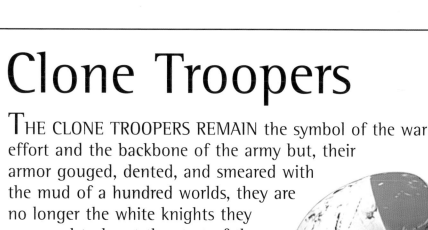

THE CLONE TROOPERS REMAIN the symbol of the war effort and the backbone of the army but, their armor gouged, dented, and smeared with the mud of a hundred worlds, they are no longer the white knights they appeared to be at the start of the war. Patched and repaired, they are returned to the front lines time and again to continue the fight for truth, justice, and, of course, the Republic way.

Helmet features built-in comlink antenna

"T" visor features heads-up display

Bodysuit glove

Shock-absorbing plastoid armor

Folding stock for braced firing

Hundreds of rounds fired on one gas cartridge

Magnatomically-sealed knee plate

DATA FILE

◆ Aging at twice the rate of normally birthed humans, only two-thirds of the original army of clone troopers are alive. Clones are also being grown on other worlds, with cells procured from new templates.

Laser cannon on Republic Star Destroyer

Despite the fact that clone armor is frequently referred to as a "body bucket," troopers think of their plastoid shell as a portable shelter, which protects them against exploding laser cannons.

Armor emblazoned with legion color

Blaster gas cartridges carried on utility belt

Action Figure

Like their clone template, Jango Fett, troopers are 1.78 meters (5 ft 10 in) tall, and their rallying cry remains: "One man, but the right man for the job!" However, three years of fighting has individualized many of the survivors. Informed by the campaigns in which they served, the wounds they sustained, and the scars they wear, troopers speak, react, and smell differently, and have acquired unique skills.

Clone troopers obey the commands of their Jedi generals, but ultimately they answer to Republic Chancellor and commander-in-chief, Palpatine. The mission to lay waste to the Jedi Temple is therefore obeyed immediately, especially as they are still being led by a Jedi Knight.

Courage, loyalty, obedience, and victory are the words that clone troopers live and die by. Though officer status was predetermined by the Kaminoans, battlefield promotions are not unknown.

Support Droids

WHEN THE KAMINOANS were growing the clone army, they also designed vessels and vehicles to bolster the troops. In making this new technology, they were guided by their thorough analysis of existing armies, such as those amassed in secret by the Trade Federation, Corporate Alliance, and Commerce Guild, and of potential planetary sectors in which sudden discord might erupt. As the war evolves and expands, taking worlds of varied climate and terrain into its dark embrace, so, too, does the need for larger ships, more powerful artillery, and a wider range of logistical and support droids.

PINCER LOADER

Bulked by multiple layers of durasteel, the IW-37 pincer— also known as the Salvager—employs its grasping arm to insert cargo or armaments into tight spaces, such as the compartment holds of Jedi interceptor starfighters.

Broadcast antennas communicate with other droids in binary

Primitive cognitive module

Remote sensor

Signal receiver

Wide-angle scanner

Large central photoreceptor

HOVER LOADER

Employed on landing platforms throughout Coruscant, hover loaders are a common feature at the Jedi Temple embarkation area, assisting in light-duty cargo relocation or, more often, droid traffic control. Hover loaders are also deployed at hyperspace ring stations to assist in the refueling of Jedi and clone-piloted starfighters.

Positioning arms

Graspers fasten to hyperspace rings

Hands made for handling cargo skids or missiles

Massive magnapod feet

Durasteel legs powered by hydraulics

DATA FILE

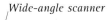

◆ The owners of Sienar Systems, Kuat Drive Yards, Baktoid Armor Workshops, and Haor Chall Engineering are paying attention to the Clone Wars, in the hope of placing themselves profitably for the inevitable peace.

Ordnance Lifter

Cybot Galactica's military version of their binary load lifter, the Ordnance Lifter stands three meters (9 ft 10 in) tall on powerful durasteel legs anchored by magnapod disks. Arms built for handling cargo skids or missiles flank a primitive cognitive module, capable of accepting verbal commands.

Utapauns

THE PEACEFUL OUTER RIM WORLD OF UTAPAU is shared by two indigenous and symbiotic near-human species. Comprising thirty percent of the population, the languid Pau'ans constitute Utapau's modest patrician class, and serve as city administrators and bureaucrats. Humble by nature, the stubby Utai make up the labor class. Unaffiliated with either the Republic or the CIS, the Utapauns remain neutral in the war until Darth Sidious sends General Grievous and the Separatist Council to their world as a temporary sanctuary. The Utapauns accept occupation with resignation, while preparing for rebellion.

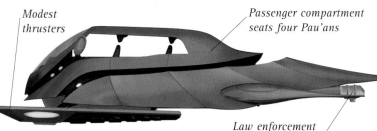

Utapau's most remote moon is inhabited

Utapau and its brood of small moons orbit in the remote Tarabba Sector. Huge sinkholes house cities that cling to the rocky walls of crevasses that fracture much of the planet's inhospitable surface.

Modest thrusters

Passenger compartment seats four Pau'ans

Law enforcement blasters are rarely used

MANKVIM 814 INTERCEPTOR
The Separatists fortify their position on Utapau by unleashing hastily-manufactured Techno Union fighters against invading Republic forces. The Mankvims are outfitted with twin laser cannons.

Shield conforms to profile

Distended eyes

LANDING PLATFORM
Obi-Wan lands in Pau City and is met by Tion Medon, who assures him that nothing strange has occurred. While Obi-Wan's Jedi Interceptor is refueled, Tion whispers that Separatists have taken control of Utapau.

Utai

Utapau's immense sinkholes were home to the Utai long before climactic change drove the lordly Pau'ans from the planet's surface. Distended eyes provide the Utai with keen night vision, perfectly suited to the crevasses that fissure Utapau. The Utai tamed the varactyl, and still serve as wranglers for the dragon mounts.

Varactyl muck boots

Mid-body ridge of spines displayed during courting ritual

Flexible neck supports armor-plated skull

Clawed feet adapted for scaling rocky cliffs

Long crooked legs

Four meters (13 ft 1 in) tall at the shoulder, the varactyl is an obliging herbivore. Utai leatherworkers handcraft high-backed saddles, sized for Pau'ans and Utai and perfect for riding at any angle.

Tion Medon

Longevity comes naturally to the Pau'ans, and Tion Medon has been Master of Port Administration for Pau City for more than 200 standard-years. A descendant of Timon Medon, who is credited with unifying Utapau, Tion Medon watches in horror as his committee members were killed by the MagnaGuards. Like all Pau'ans, Tion Medon prefers darkness to sunlight, and raw meat to cooked.

Front sight

Primitive igniter housing

Hand-turned recharge valve

Priming mechanism

ZENOTI ARMS HB-9

Ornate stock and shoulder brace

Staff fashioned from exotic alloy

Wide belt supports bony frame

Port master's walking stick

Cascade design harkens back to Pau'an relocation

Floor-length robes are a recent fashion

LAMPAY FAY
Medon's aide-de-camp also hails from an eminent lineage, the patriarch of which was among the first to encourage interstellar trade.

Double rows of teeth

Scarlet offsets for bloodless skin

Vestigial ears

Skin color result of underground living and raw meat diet

DATA FILE

◆ Because of the porous nature of Utapau's rocky mantle, surface water is scarce, but water is abundant on the floor of many of the sinkholes.

◆ The Pau'an language once had many dialects, and conflicts were common among subsurface cities.

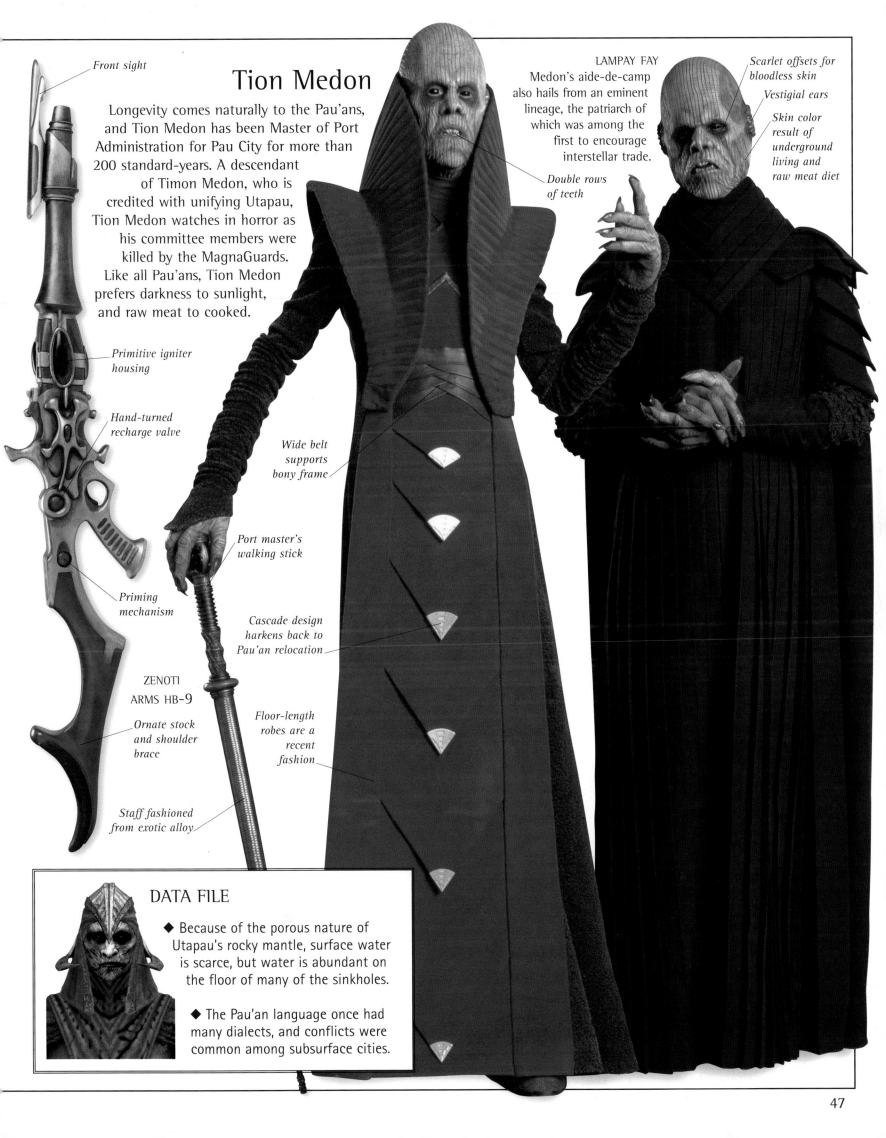

Chewbacca

COMPARATIVELY SHORT, EVEN SLIGHT, for a Wookiee, 200-year-old Chewbacca was born in the city of Rwookrrorro, several hundred kilometers from Kachirho, in an area of exceptionally tall wroshyr trees. His mother, father, and several cousins still reside there. A mechanic, holo-game competitor, and catamaran and fluttercraft pilot, Chewbacca learned his skills at Rwookrrorro's landing pad, and helped design and build the Wookiee escape pods. When it comes to outwitting droids or clone troopers, Chewbacca is ready with a plan.

Arms raised in gesture of dismay

Kashyyyk is distant from Coruscant, but close enough to hyperlanes to serve as a way-station for merchants. The Wookiees trade precious hardwoods for technology.

Wookiee Explorer

Chewbacca has explored his homeworld from pole to pole, and is acquainted with even the wildest reaches of Kashyyyk's phenomenal forests. Restless by nature, he has also visited scores of planets, and is a veteran of numerous adventures, including run-ins with Trandoshan slavers. More compassionate than fierce, he nevertheless proves himself an able and cunning warrior.

Ammunition bandoleer

On the ground and on Kachirho's loftiest tree platforms, Wookiees gaze into the night sky, which the ships of the Separatist fleet have strewn with harsh light. Chewbacca is no stranger to combat, but he worries that Kashyyyk may not be able to defend itself against the invasion force, and will fall to the Confederacy.

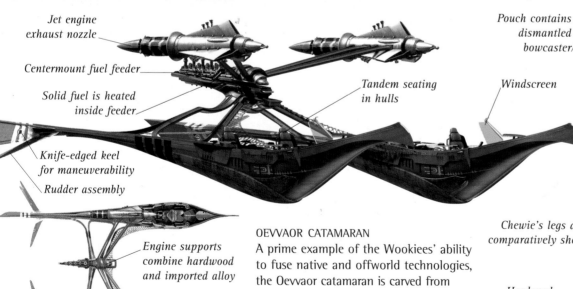

Jet engine exhaust nozzle

Centermount fuel feeder

Solid fuel is heated inside feeder

Tandem seating in hulls

Windscreen

Knife-edged keel for maneuverability

Rudder assembly

Engine supports combine hardwood and imported alloy

Pouch contains dismantled bowcaster

Chewie's legs are comparatively short

Hardened footpads from exploring Kashyyyk

TOP VIEW

OEVVAOR CATAMARAN
A prime example of the Wookiees' ability to fuse native and offworld technologies, the Oevvaor catamaran is carved from water-resistant hardwood, and driven by a pair of powerful engines. Sought by rich buyers, no two catamarans are the same, and many have lasted for a millennium.

DATA FILE

◆ Chewbacca will have his revenge on the Empire with the death of the Emperor and the destruction of the second Death Star during the battle of Endor. Jointly commanded by Chewbacca and General Han Solo, an Alliance task force will restore peace to Kashyyyk.

Immense lung capacity required to sound call

ELDER'S STAFF

KASHYYYK CLARION

Hammered bronzium jacket inlaid with cerulean gemstone

Wood is over six centuries old

MASTER CARVERS

Wookiees turn their dexterous hands to carving at an early age, fashioning household items, musical instruments, and tools. The Kashyyyk clarion is made from the horn of a bantha, and jacketed with hand-hammered bronzium.

Mouth emits bellow that can be heard for 20 kilometers (12 miles)

Elaborately engraved stem

CEREMONIAL PIPE

Fangs puncture even durable Trandoshan skin

Respected elder

Wookiees are prized by slavers as much for their strong backs as for their keen intellects. Resourceful and fiercely loyal, Wookiees do not live as long as some species, but several residents of Kachirho and Rwookrrorro can recall when Yoda was a mere Jedi Knight.

Emblem of the Kachirho clan

Wookiees can pull a person's arm from its socket

Water-shedding hair covers Wookiees like a cape

The Gathering

The clarion call to defend Kachirho summons young and old, from all areas of Kashyyyk. Despite the victory at the tree-city, Kashyyyk will became enslaved to the Empire soon after the end of the Clone Wars, and thousands of Wookiees, including Chewbacca, will be exported to remote worlds to serve as laborers. Even captivity, however, will not dampen Chewbacca's abiding fondness for humans.

GUANTA

LACHICHUK

MERUMERU

Tarfful

TARFFUL HAS SERVED AS LEADER of the Wookiee city of Kachirho for longer than a human lifetime. He has already experienced captivity, having fallen into the clawed hands of Trandoshan slavers who have long been enemies of the Wookiees, and who had cut a deal with Count Dooku. Standing over two meters (seven feet) tall, Tarfful is literally looked up to by many, and so assumes the role of commander when Separatist forces invade.

Unlike most areas of Kashyyyk, where the wroshyrs tower so high above the surface that Wookiees seldom leave their tree-caves, Kachirho rises from the shore of a large fresh-water lagoon.

Locks of hair banded by precious metal rings

Decorative pauldron

Kashyyyk long-gun heat dissipater

Ferocious visage

Teeth bared for war cry

Clan pectoral cinches crossed bandoleers

Orb-igniter

Tarfful is left-handed

Shield depicts emblem of Kachirho

Stylized eyespots of Kashyyyk borer beetle

Kashyyyk Landing

Tarfful is well-known on the planet of Kashyyyk. When word spreads that Kachirho is under siege by the Confederacy's droid forces, Wookiees from throughout the region hurry to defend the arboreal city, which gracefully spirals around the trunk of a 300-meter (984-feet) high wroshyr tree.

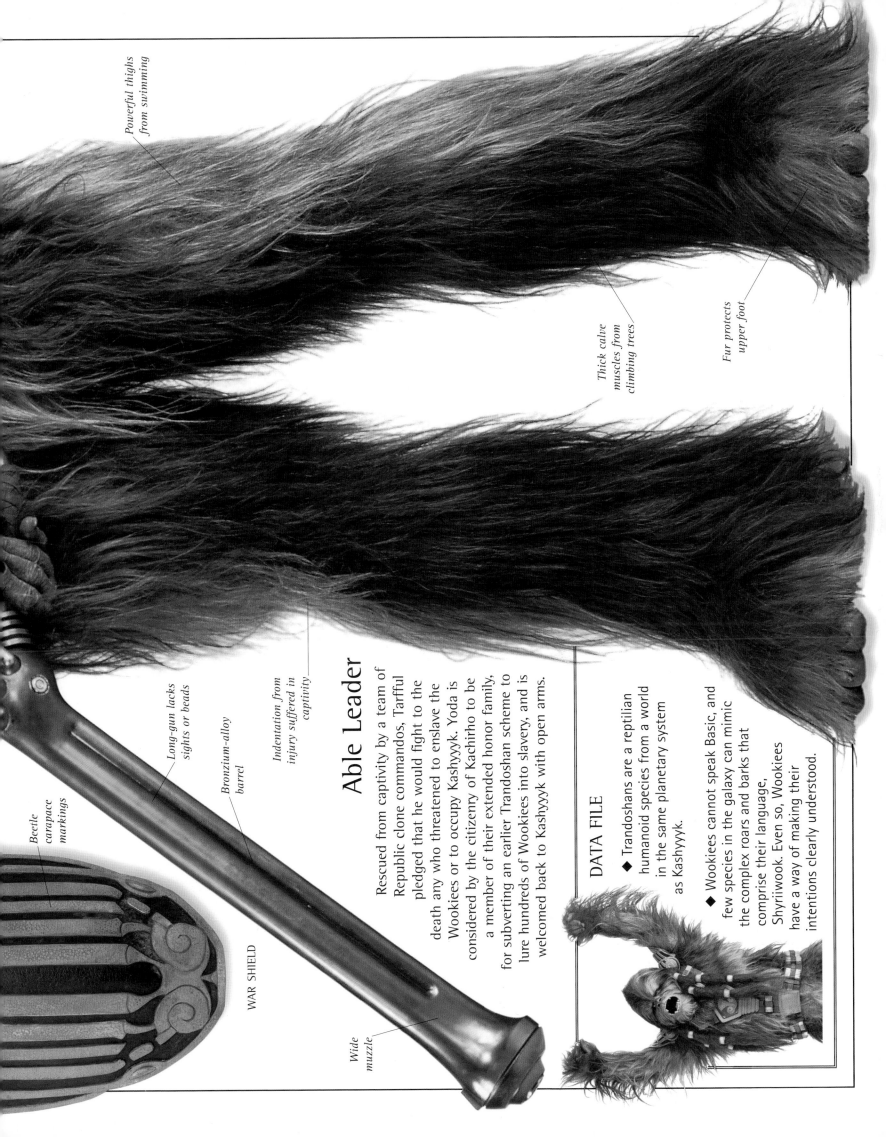

Powerful thighs from swimming

Thick calve muscles from climbing trees

Fur protects upper foot

Beetle carapace markings

Long-gun lacks sights or beads

Bronzium-alloy barrel

Indentation from injury suffered in captivity

WAR SHIELD

Wide muzzle

Able Leader

Rescued from captivity by a team of Republic clone commandos, Tarfful pledged that he would fight to the death any who threatened to enslave the Wookiees or to occupy Kashyyyk. Yoda is considered by the citizenry of Kachirho to be a member of their extended honor family, for subverting an earlier Trandoshan scheme to lure hundreds of Wookiees into slavery, and is welcomed back to Kashyyyk with open arms.

DATA FILE

◆ Trandoshans are a reptilian humanoid species from a world in the same planetary system as Kashyyyk.

◆ Wookiees cannot speak Basic, and few species in the galaxy can mimic the complex roars and barks that comprise their language, Shyriiwook. Even so, Wookiees have a way of making their intentions clearly understood.

Wookiee Weapons

THE WOOKIEE LANGUAGE contains over 150 words for wood, many of them devoted to grain, moisture content, and factors that can influence warping, twisting, and checking. Shipboard logs cite instances of Wookiees effecting temporary repairs of starship drives using pieces of wood. Commentators have classified even their blasters as "art," and yet the language has no word for "artist." Wookiees view their innate talents for carving and engraving as mere survival skills.

KLORRI-CLAN BATTLE SHIELD
Carved with symbolic motifs and banded with bronzium, the two thousand-year-old Klorri-clan battle shields are normally displayed only during important rituals and ceremonies.

Blaster gas cartridges

PAULDRON

Crest is ancient sun symbol

Hair can be threaded through perforated flange

HELMET

MILITARY WEAR
Armor, harnesses, and other examples of military gear evolved from ceremonial clan regalia, in the same way that most Wookiee implements of war have their origin in hunting. Halter and shoulder-slung bandoleers typically hold power packs, blaster gas canisters, and bowcaster quarrels.

AMMO HALTER

Polarizer

Bowcaster

The traditional bowcaster still enjoys wide use as a ranged weapon. The original bowcaster had few metal parts, and employed a length of braided kshyy vine to fire a wooden quarrel. The stock was adorned with clan or tree-city emblems, or inlaid with semi-precious stones or mosaics of contrasting hardwood.

Stock is tapered for line-of-sight accuracy

Battery pack is mortised into stock

Rear sight

Bowstring catch

Tensile bowstring

Blaster gas lines

BOWCASTER MECHANICS
The bowcaster works on the principle of magnetic acceleration. A pair of spherical polarizers generate positive and negative pulses that power the weapon's tensile metal bowstring. Enveloped in energy when it emerges from the barrel, the quarrel could be mistaken for a blaster bolt.

Ribbed launch shaft

Conduction chamber housed in shaft

Metal bowstring

Barrel

Front sight

Power pack

Stock recoil spring

Safety catch

Conduction chamber

Magnetic acceleration coil

Trigger

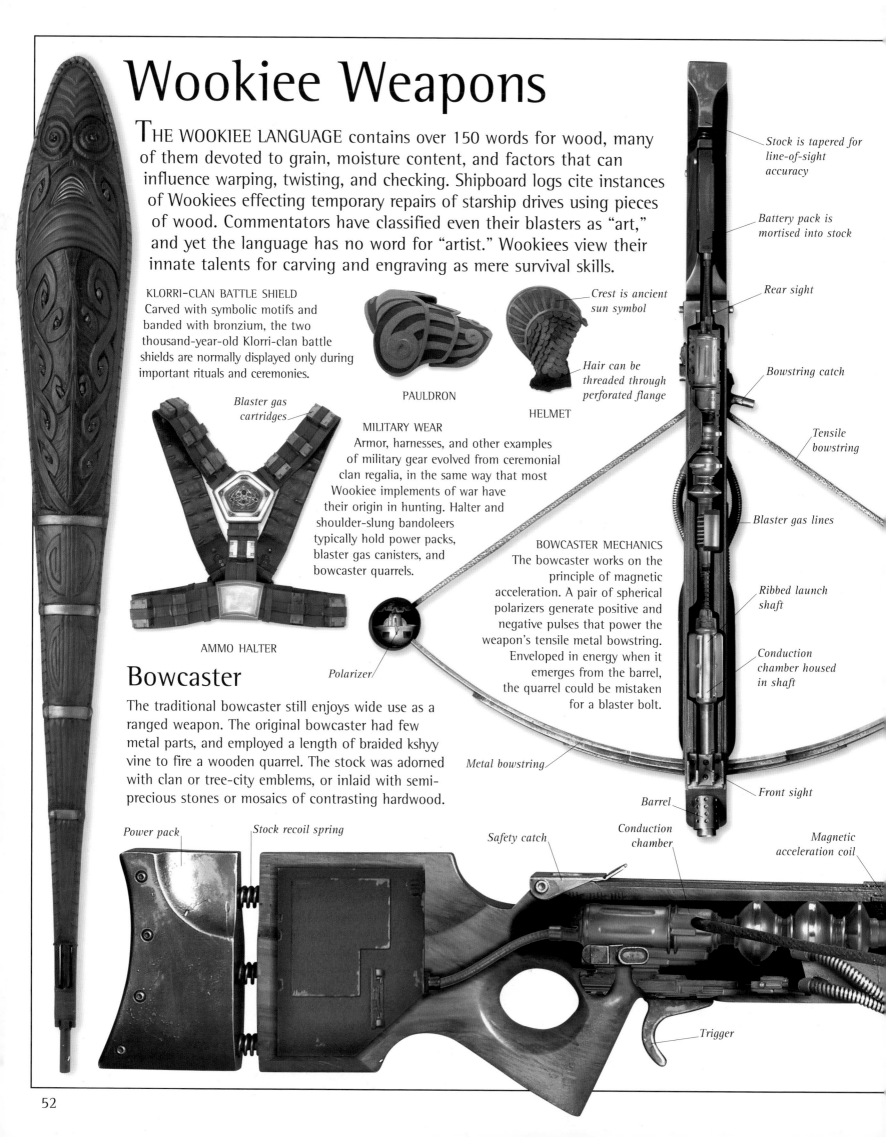

◆ The Battle of Kachirho might not have gone as well for the Wookiees had Yoda not been there to lend his lightsaber to the fray. Similarly, the battle might not have gone as well for Yoda had the Wookiees not peppered the area around the tree-city with launch-capable escape pods, in case Kachirho had to be evacuated.

Sure-Shot

Tremendous strength is required to cock and control bowcasters. Traveling circuses use bowcasters in feats-of-strength competitions. Chewbacca's, however, is more tribute than traditional, with an automatic recocking system and low-light scope. Consequently, his bandoleer houses more power packs than most.

Ring-grip peculiar to southern hemisphere tree-cities

DISRUPTOR

Bronzium alloy blast suppressor

Accelerator

SIDE-ARM

BLASTERS

Of the array of blasters fashioned by Wookiee weaponsmiths, several models are favorites and are now mass-produced in workshops all over Kashyyyk. Blaster technology has influenced traditional weapons as well, with the over-under bowcaster featuring a built-in blaster.

Bowcaster easily dismantled

Automatic recocking system

Polarizers positioned forward of barrel

Quarrel autofeed mechanism

Shortened stock

CHEWBACCA'S BOWCASTER

SLUG-THROWER

Blaster gas cartridges

Polarizer

Electromagnetic coil for ultra-power blasts

Front sight

Barrel

Lowered rear sight

Bail Organa

Sheltay Retrac has been Bail's aide for two years

Alderaanian long coat

Wool produced in Alderaan's Killik region

SENATOR FOR PACIFIC ALDERAAN, Bail Organa believes that the peace he enjoys on his homeworld may account for his growing concerns about the conflict on Coruscant. He is particularly concerned about the extra powers the Senate has given to Chancellor Palpatine and the loss of freedom on the galactic capital. Bail is seen as a voice of reason in the Senate, although just as often he is shouted down by his pro-war peers.

When Palpatine proclaims himself Emperor, Padmé cautions Bail to conceal his true feelings. She asks him to bide his time until the circumstances are right. Most of all, in private, she tells him to place his faith in the future and in the Force.

Candid Senator

With Padmé, Mon Mothma, Fang Zar, and other Loyalists, Bail argued against the Military Creation Act, only to put aside his feelings after the Battle of Geonosis and support the war effort. To no avail, Bail argued against the installation of surveillance holocams in the Senate Building and, later, against the Reflex Amendment that extended Palpatine's far-reaching authority.

BAIL ORGANA'S IDENTITY TAG

Blaster fires incapacitating bolts only

TARGET BLASTER
Bail has grown used to showing his identity tag at building entrances on Coruscant. Seemingly passive, his resoluteness will be passed on to his adopted daughter.

Friend of the Jedi

Bail knew several Jedi Masters before the start of the war. Since then, he has gotten to know them even better. Bail meets often with Yoda and Mace Windu to discuss Palpatine's use of Republic forces and the growing mistrust of the Jedi Order in the Republic. He understands more than most that the war has placed the Jedi in an impossible situation.

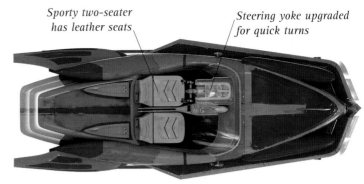

Sporty two-seater has leather seats

Steering yoke upgraded for quick turns

CUSTOM SPEEDER
With its design based on an older model, Bail's speeder comes in handy for spiriting Yoda to safety after he abandons the fight with Darth Sidious in the Senate building.

Bail believes in the Force and is the first civilian to arrive at the Jedi Temple after Anakin and his legion of clone troopers have gone on a killing spree. After witnessing a young Jedi fall to hails of blaster fire, Bail narrowly escapes with his own life.

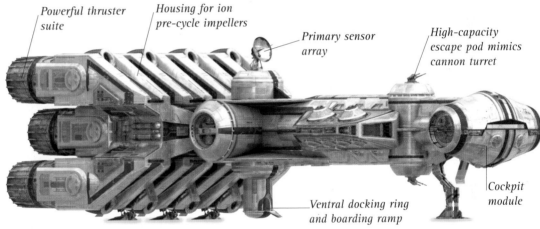

Powerful thruster suite

Housing for ion pre-cycle impellers

Primary sensor array

High-capacity escape pod mimics cannon turret

Cockpit module

Ventral docking ring and boarding ramp

DIPLOMATIC STARSHIP
Bail's Corellian-made cruiser, *Tantive IV*, is commanded by Captain Raymus Antilles. In order to preserve its legacy as a diplomatic vessel, Bail refuses to outfit the ship with ranged weapons. On and off for the next 20 years, the starship will be home to C-3PO and R2-D2.

To keep the whereabouts of Obi-Wan and Yoda secret after they have gone into exile, Bail orders that C-3PO's memory be wiped.

DATA FILE

◆ Bail will die when Grand Moff Tarkin orders the Death Star to destroy Alderaan.

◆ Using a Jedi homing beacon, Bail is able to contact Yoda and Obi-Wan after they are betrayed by clone commanders Gree and Cody.

◆ Bail and his wife, Breha, are childless.

Overcome by grief for what has transpired since the kidnap of Palpatine, Bail watches medtechs at the Polis Massa facility struggle to save Padmé's life after they have delivered her twins. After her death, Bail offers to raise Leia Amidala Skywalker in the house of his wife, the Queen of Alderaan.

Separatist Council

EARLY IN THE WAR, following the Separatists' first round of conquests, Count Dooku revealed to the Council members that the real power behind the Confederacy of Independent Systems was the Sith Lord, Darth Sidious. Three years later during the Outer Rim Sieges, with the Republic victorious at Separatist strongholds, Sidious orders that the Council members be placed under the personal protection of General Grievous. Housed on Utapau while Grievous strikes at Coruscant, the Council is then relocated to volcanic Mustafar.

The "hive mentality" characteristic of many of the Separatists works in Sidious's favor, in that once a leader is won over, the rest of his or her species follows. Their spinelessness makes it easier for the Sith Lord to order the murder of his former allies.

Cranial crown

PASSEL ARGENTE

WAT TAMBOR

Vocabular/ annunciator

Hides within oily Koorivan cloak

DENARIA KEE (AIDE)

Attitude of prayer

SHI'IDO (AIDE)

Elaborate breast plate doubles as body armor

PO NUDO

Tusks

Primary Aqualish eyes

TECHNO UNION
Wat Tambor has suffered several close calls during the war, falling into Republic captivity on Metalorn and narrowly escaping an assassination attempt by Boba Fett on Xagobah. With his homeworld of Skako in Republic hands, Tambor has no option but to place his trust in Sidious.

CORPORATE ALLIANCE
Passel Argente had hoped to play a secondary role in the war, but quickly found himself pressed into service by Dooku. Unknown to Passel, many of his Alliance subordinates have been relocating their distribution companies to a cluster of star systems in the galaxy's Tingel Arm, also known as the Corporate Sector.

HYPER-COMMUNICATIONS CARTEL
Aqualish Po Nudo helped to influence dozens of unscrupulous Senators and steered resource-rich Ando into the Separatist fold in the months prior to the Battle of Geonosis. In gratitude, the Banking Clan and the Techno Union appointed him head of the Hyper-Communications Cartel. This organization oversees a CIS analogue of the Republic HoloNet.

Endgame

The Separatist facility on volcanic Mustafar was thought to be impregnable. But that was before Darth

Sidious sent his new apprentice, Darth Vader, to assassinate the members of the Council. With the Jedi killed, and the chief Separatists soon to follow, no one will stand in Sidious's and Vader's way when they seize total control of the galaxy.

DATA FILE

◆ The Separatist movement ignored all Republic laws prohibiting the amassing of weapons, warships, and soldiers.

◆ The Separatists prevented Republic eavesdropping by using an InterGalactic Banking Clan code.

SAN HILL

Strong neck muscles support heavy cranium

Troubled posture

Heritage miter

RUNE HAAKO

Cato Neimoidian yoke collar

Now paralyzed wings folded behind back

ARCHDUKE POGGLE THE LESSER

NUTE GUNRAY

Command headdress

CAT MIIN (AIDE)

SHU MAI

Neck rings

BANKING CLAN
San Hill was taken into Republic custody and allowed to escape. Having financed the resurrection of the Gen'dai warrior Durge, as well as the rehabilitation of Grievous, Hill feels that Darth Sidious owes him a great debt.

GEONOSIAN INDUSTRIES
With hundreds of thousands of his fellow Geonosians employed in the construction of Darth Sidious's battle station, Poggle the Lesser is confident that the best is yet to come.

TRADE FEDERATION
More than any other members of the Council, the Neimoidian Viceroy, Nute Gunray, and his chief attaché, Rune Haako, feel they have a special agreement with Darth Sidious. This is mainly because the Trade Federation was the first organization to be drawn into helping the Sith Lord's evil plans.

COMMERCE GUILD
With her homeworld of Castell absorbed into the Republic, Gossam Presidente Shu Mai's talent for bribery is useless against Vader.

Polis Massans

MYSTERY SURROUNDS THE CAUSE of the cataclysm that fractured the Outer Rim planet now known as Polis Massa. Evidence of the civilization that flourished on the formerly arid world is scant, but on one of the largest of the planetary chunks, an archaeological dig has been in progress for so long that the humanoid aliens supervising the dig are themselves referred to as Polis Massans. Most of the prize artifacts uncovered thus far have come from deep within the asteroid, and so seasoned spelunkers—cavers—comprise the majority of the archaeological team. The medical facility to which Padmé is taken was built primarily to suit the needs of the investigators. Known for their discretion, the Polis Massans ask few questions of Bail or the Jedi Masters.

Obi-Wan, Padmé, R2-D2, and C-3PO rendezvous with Yoda and Bail Organa at the Polis Massa medical facility. The fact that the facility is remote suits the purposes of the Jedi, who are determined to keep secret the birth of Padmé's children. The medtechs who assist in delivering the twins are baffled by their inability to save her life. But sometimes a broken heart simply cannot be mended.

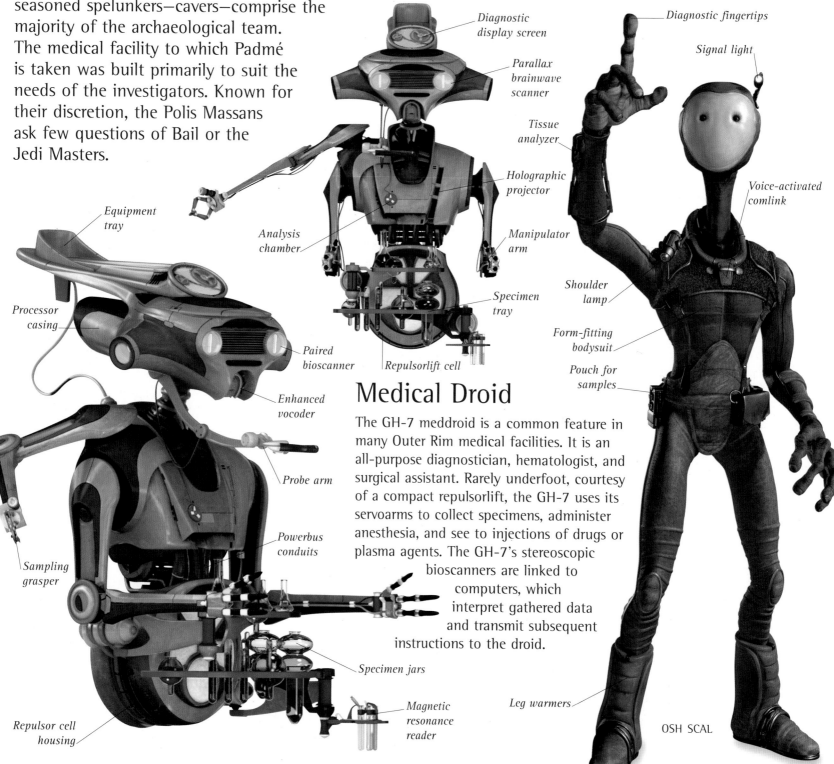

Diagnostic display screen

Parallax brainwave scanner

Tissue analyzer

Holographic projector

Manipulator arm

Equipment tray

Analysis chamber

Specimen tray

Processor casing

Paired bioscanner

Repulsorlift cell

Enhanced vocoder

Probe arm

Powerbus conduits

Sampling grasper

Specimen jars

Repulsor cell housing

Magnetic resonance reader

Diagnostic fingertips

Signal light

Voice-activated comlink

Shoulder lamp

Form-fitting bodysuit

Pouch for samples

Leg warmers

OSH SCAL

Medical Droid

The GH-7 meddroid is a common feature in many Outer Rim medical facilities. It is an all-purpose diagnostician, hematologist, and surgical assistant. Rarely underfoot, courtesy of a compact repulsorlift, the GH-7 uses its servoarms to collect specimens, administer anesthesia, and see to injections of drugs or plasma agents. The GH-7's stereoscopic bioscanners are linked to computers, which interpret gathered data and transmit subsequent instructions to the droid.

MIDWIFE DROID

Non-threatening aspect

Warming cushion

The current Polis Massan team has had limited contact with humans, and knows little about delivering human children. After consulting their databanks, the medtechs select as midwife a padded droid, equipped with a thermal cushion and paddle appendages with which to cradle the newborns.

Nutrient reservoir

Repulsorlift

Cradling paddle

Fearing the worst for Padmé, Bail orders Captain Antilles to delete all data about Mustafar from Padmé's starship computer. With Anakin believed dead, Bail wonders what the Jedi will do with the twins, whom Padmé has named Luke and Leia.

Head lamp

Deep-focus eyes

Droid summoner

Mildly telepathic brain

Sign language gesture

Osmotic membrane face

Surgical hood

Remote control

Caver's harness

Surgical hood seal

Sample containers

Alien Medics

Only two of the technicians that help deliver the Skywalker twins are trained physicians. The rest are exobiolologists, natives of a Subterrel sector world. They are attached to the archaeological team to analyze artifacts for organic tissue, suitable for cloning. Padmé's condition is judged to be so critical that the techs have no time to change out of their caving jumpsuits.

Utility belt

Remote control unit

Warming line

Suit reveals body growth-rings

Knee pads

DZNORI XAM

SELIF XAM

MANEELI TUUN

Darth Sidious

THE SITH HAVE WAITED a millennium for the birth of one who is powerful enough to return them from hiding. Darth Sidious is that one—the Sith's revenge on the Jedi order for having nearly eradicated the practitioners of the dark side of the Force. Trained by Darth Plagueis, Sidious, in his guise as Palpatine, understood that the corrupt Republic and the subservient Jedi Order could be brought down by playing to the weaknesses of the former: its mindless bureaucracy and attachment to power.

Sith hood and mantle

Face deformed by Sith lightning

Sidious does not consider himself evil but rather a savior. After the destruction of the Jedi order, he has no need to reveal his Sith identity, for he is now the beloved Emperor Palpatine, who has restored peace to the galaxy.

Sidious has one more task to perform before his conquest is complete: to kill Yoda. Then the light side of the Force will be eclipsed, and the Jedi order will cease to exist.

Precious aurodium cap and blade emitter

Phrik alloy casing

Blade-length adjust

Voluminous Sith robes

LIGHTSABER
Sidious's Sith lightsaber is usually concealed within a neuranium sculpture that adorns his chambers in the Senate Office Building. A wall panel in the office depicts a legendary battle between the Sith and the Jedi.

Two Faces

"Always two there are"—not only master and apprentice, but persona and true face. Unmasked by deflected lightning during his duel with Mace Windu, the Sith Lord's true face is revealed to the world. But for the Senate, the Jedi could not damage Palpatine's reputation.

DATA FILE

◆ A powerful practitioner of the dark side of the Force, Sidious uses Sith lightning to attack his enemies. It causes terrible pain.

◆ Sidious's act as the mild-mannered Chancellor Palpatine is so convincing that even the Jedi are taken in.

Darth Vader will represent the Sith, serving as Palpatine's liaison with the planetary system governors he has installed. He will also keep the military commanders in line—at least until work is completed on the Death Star.

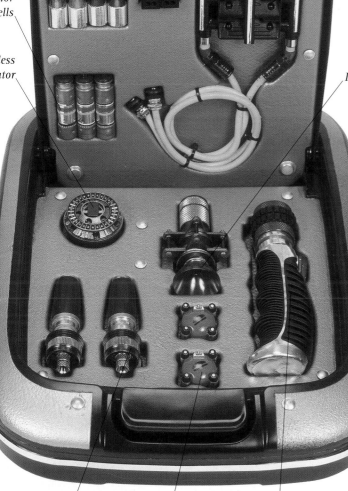

Vials of injectable bacta and bota

Injector power cells

Wireless defibrilator

Filtration transpirators

Resuscitating ventilator

Sith lightsaber

Injector head

Medical Kit

Plucked from death on the black-sand bank of one of Mustafar's lava rivers, Darth Vader is placed in a medical capsule that will keep him alive during the hyperspace jump to Coruscant. Along the way, Darth Sidious makes use of various special potions and implements to begin the process of Darth Vader's transformation into the man-machine he is destined to become.

Face has turned yellow in anger

Adaptors for pressor field generator

Cardiovascular monitors

Injector handle

Sith Lord

Darth Sidious isn't worried about any Jedi who managed to survive Order 66. Even united, Yoda and Obi-Wan pose no threat to the Dark Lords of the Sith. Soon the Jedi will be remembered only as archaic warriors, practicing a sad religion, and memories of the Republic will disappear. For Sidious, everything is proceeding according to plan.

Emperor Palpatine's shuttle can jump to lightspeed without having to use a hyperspace ring. The same is true of the V-wings that form his special escort.

Dark robes hide Sidious's identity

Darth Vader

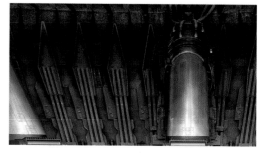

FOLLOWING THE ATROCITIES he commits on Coruscant, Darth Vader is sent to Mustafar to "take care of the Separatist Council." There, he carries out his task with homicidal glee, executing one member after the next, saving an imploring Nute Gunray for last. His bloodlust temporarily sated, Vader learns that Padmé has followed him across the stars. But when she rebuffs his offer to rule the galaxy at his side, and it is revealed that Obi-Wan has accompanied her, Vader nearly chokes his wife to death with the Force, before engaging his former Master in a deadly duel above the planet's rivers of lava.

MUSTAFAR
Intended to shelter the Separatist Council while the final acts of the Clone Wars are played out, the facility on Mustafar ends up being a costly grave for the hoodwinked half-dozen Separatists who funded its construction.

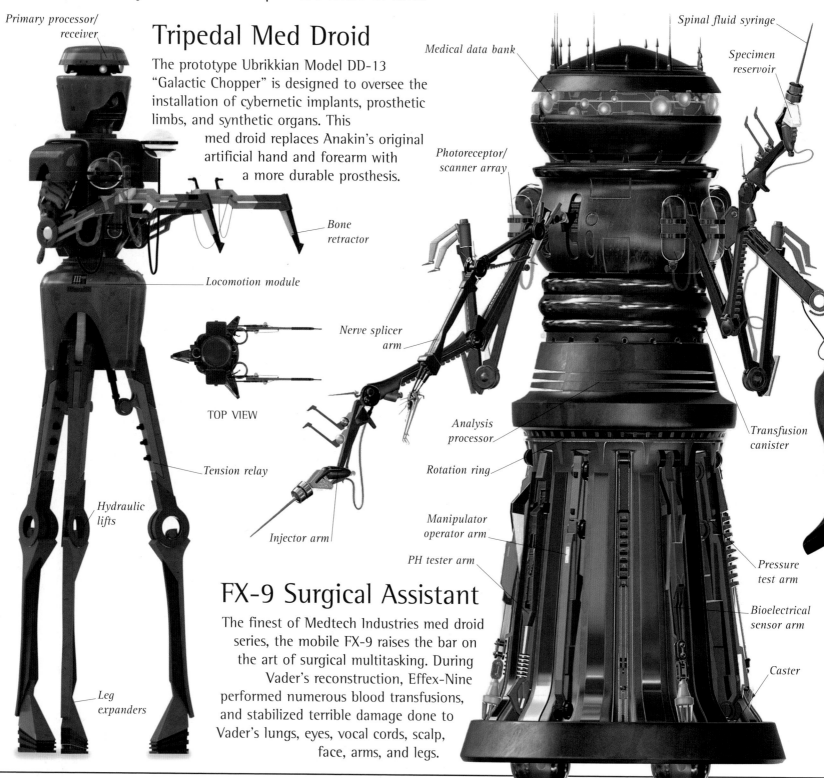

Primary processor/ receiver

Tripedal Med Droid

The prototype Ubrikkian Model DD-13 "Galactic Chopper" is designed to oversee the installation of cybernetic implants, prosthetic limbs, and synthetic organs. This med droid replaces Anakin's original artificial hand and forearm with a more durable prosthesis.

Medical data bank

Spinal fluid syringe

Specimen reservoir

Photoreceptor/ scanner array

Bone retractor

Locomotion module

Nerve splicer arm

TOP VIEW

Analysis processor

Transfusion canister

Tension relay

Rotation ring

Injector arm

Hydraulic lifts

Manipulator operator arm

PH tester arm

Pressure test arm

FX-9 Surgical Assistant

The finest of Medtech Industries med droid series, the mobile FX-9 raises the bar on the art of surgical multitasking. During Vader's reconstruction, Effex-Nine performed numerous blood transfusions, and stabilized terrible damage done to Vader's lungs, eyes, vocal cords, scalp, face, arms, and legs.

Bioelectrical sensor arm

Caster

Leg expanders

Dark Lord of the Sith

Awakened from his life-altering reconstruction on a gleaming table in Sidious's laboratory, Anakin learns that Padmé is dead—most likely by his own hand. His subsequent scream destroys nearly everything in the lab, including most of the med droids. The realization that he has killed the person he loved most will haunt him for the rest of his life.

Voice projector/ respiratory intake

Locking helmet

Vision enhancement receptors

Hermetic collar

Control function panel

Bloodshine Sith blade

Sith crystal chamber

Power indicator

Activator

Blade power adjuster

Plastoid girdle protects abdominal organs

NEW LIGHTSABER
Vader will build a new lightsaber, powered by a synth-crystal supplied by Sidious that will yield a crimson blade.

Function indicators

SYSTEMS STATUS BELT

Laser scalpel arm

System function display

DATA FILE

◆ As a result of having artificial arms, Darth Vader will never be able to conjure Sith lightning—nor be invulnerable to it.

◆ After Palpatine's creation of the Empire, academies for the training of non-clone Imperial officers will appear.

Ribbed multi-ply trousers

Shin armor protects prosthesis

While Sidious is pleased to find that Anakin's rage has survived intact, Darth Vader is not what Sidious was expecting, and not the perfect apprentice to perpetuate the legacy of the Sith.

Boots adhere to artificial limb

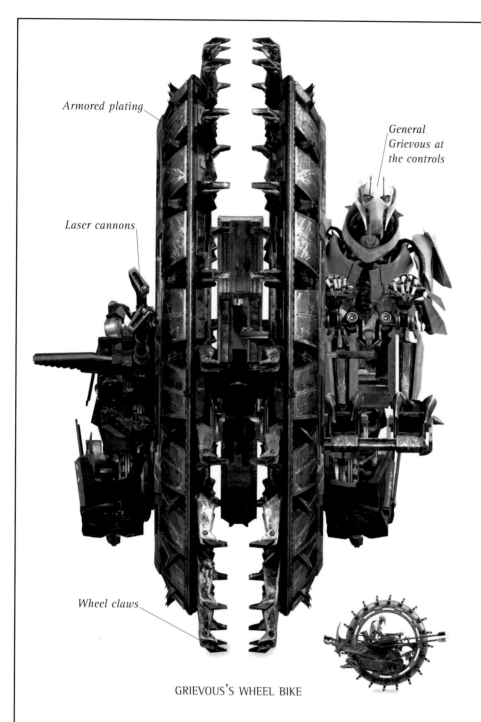

Armored plating

General Grievous at the controls

Laser cannons

Wheel claws

GRIEVOUS'S WHEEL BIKE

LONDON, NEW YORK, MELBOURNE, MUNICH, and DELHI

DORLING KINDERSLEY

PROJECT ART EDITOR Dan Bunyan
EDITOR Laura Gilbert
PUBLISHING MANAGER Simon Beecroft
ART DIRECTOR Mark Richards
CATEGORY PUBLISHER Alex Kirkham
DTP DESIGNER Lauren Egan
PRODUCTION Rochelle Talary

LUCASFILM LTD.

ART EDITOR Iain R. Morris
SENIOR EDITOR Jonathan W. Rinzler
CONTINUITY SUPERVISOR Leland Chee

First published in Great Britain in 2005 by
Dorling Kindersley Limited,
80 Strand, London WC2R 0RL

05 06 07 08 09 10 9 8 7 6 5 4 3 2

A CIP catalogue record for this book is available from the British Library.

ISBN 1-4053-0827-3

Color reproduction by Media Development and Printing Ltd, UK
Printed and bound in Italy by L.E.G.O.

Acknowledgements

As in any project of this sort, contributions came from all quarters, sometimes too fast and furious to keep up with, though I think we managed to squeeze everything in. So, many thanks to the following contributors:

Jonathan Rinzler, not only for his editorial work, but also for sharing some of his experiences in writing *The Making of Revenge of the Sith*; Iain Morris, for steering us to the best film stills and artwork, and training his keen eye on the page layouts; Amy Gary and Stacey Cheregotis, also of Lucas Licensing, for their support, encouragement, and guidance; Pablo Hidalgo and Steve Sansweet, for recounting some of the conversations they had with actors and others; Leland Chee, for his help in getting the details right; Concept Design Supervisor, Ryan Church, and ILM Art Directors Aaron McBride and

Alex Jaeger, for taking time out of their busy schedules to talk to us about early concepts for characters and settings and what they eventually grew into; Ryan Kaufman and Justin Lambros, of LucasArts, for leading us through the many and extraordinary levels of the *Revenge of the Sith* and Republic Commando games; Warren Fu, concept designer of Grievous, for supplying additional information about the origins of the cyborg general; sculptor Robert Barnes, who created the Grievous cutaway, and modelmaker John Goodson, who constructed the Wookiee bowcaster and Sith medical kit, and Alex Ivanov, who photographed all three; Curtis Saxton, for sharing the texts he wrote for DK's *Star Wars: Revenge of the Sith Incredible Cross-Sections*; and Matt Stover, whose adaptation of the film is indispensable for seeing more deeply into characters and events.

Finally, special thanks to my agent, Eleanor Wood, of Spectrum Literary Agency, and to three people at Dorling Kindersley, without whom the project wouldn't have pulled together: Laura Gilbert, for her careful edits and inspired tweaks; and project supervisor Simon Beecroft and designer Dan Bunyan, who made a week of focused work at Big Rock Ranch seem more like a vacation. Let's raise a glass of pale to the Manager's Reception, lads!

DK Publishing would also like to thank: Neil Kelly and Kate Simkins for additional editorial help.